LIFE PIRATE

A POEM COLLECTION ON LIFE, DEATH & ALL THAT JAZZ

By Chris Statham

Also By

THE UGLY GLORY SERIES

THE MAN IN THE MIRROR - A collection on male mental health
FRIDAY NIGHT FEVER – A collection on booze, nightlife & the battle with sobriety
JELLIED EELS & MULTI-CULTURALISM – A collection on modern life in the UK
THIS IS WHY WE MET - A collection on dating, friends with benefits & sex workers
MY NORTH STAR - A collection on love, divorce & finding a way forward
JUST ANOTHER MARTIAN CAT LIVING IN BASILDON - A collection on exploring creativity & the world
LIFE PIRATE – A collection on life, death & all that jazz

AFRONIA SERIES

Crying for Afronia (Volume 1)
Escape from Afronia (Volume 2)
Dying for Afronia (Volume 3)
Afronia Rising (Volume 4)
Developing Afronia (Volume 5)

PROSE, POEM AND PICTURES SERIES

7 Days in 1 Week (Volume 1)
12 Months in a Year (Volume 2)
10 Years in a Decade (Volume 3)

OTHER FICTION NOVELS

18 Reflections and 3 Statements of Relief
Paperback Writer

DEDICATION

To my fellow life pirates, you know who you are!

Copyright and Disclaimer

Author – Chris Statham
Sketches by Hezdean Chinthengah
Published by **www.creativityxroads.com**
Life Pirate, 978-1-9161867-7-4

CONTENTS

FORWARD

I am a middle-aged man from the UK and in the process of losing three generations of my family. My father passed away two months ago, divorce proceedings started one month ago, and most likely my children will live overseas once everything pans out. This is without a doubt the hardest part of my life journey I've so far had to manage.

I can still remember black and white TV, coal fires, outdoor toilets and the ubiquitous red telephone and post box at the end of the street. Growing up I would stay in a B'n'B rather than rent a person's flat through AirBnB. If I wanted a taxi, I would dial for a minicab not swipe for an Uber. I would record TV or watch films on video cassettes rather than downloads. I would put printed photos in an album or make a collage, not upload onto Snapchat, Facebook or one of the many other social media platforms. I would look in the dictionary or Encyclopaedia Britannica if I wanted some information rather than rely on the Google god. And don't get me started on fitbits, bitcoins and emojis and which have left me somewhat bewildered.

As a child of the 80's, I remember when Madonna subversively sang about being a virgin and, Frankie controversially went to Hollywood. I have memories of Christmases past, present, and think of future ones, the echo in my mind, reminiscent of Scrooge's night-time encounters with the ghost of Jacob Marley. I think of when I was a youngster, happy days. Then teenager years of loneliness. In my 20s, life was for living. 30s I was celebrating Christmas with my kids, but now, this Christmas I will be by myself. Who knows what future Christmases will bring when I'm an old duffer.

From child to parent, this is what getting older is, what growing up means. You have to accept responsibilities and be accountable for actions. I now understand that life doesn't revolve around my happiness, but of those who I'm answerable to. The future remains a mystery, and I am uncertain about the possibilities that lie ahead. I don't know if will once more have a babe cradled in my arms, twins or I will be sterile. Maybe, I will live out my days in solitude.

This is the journey of life, birthdays and Christmases unmoveable markers, constants of personal reality in a changing world. As years pass, we gain wisdom and insights about the world and ourselves. What we thought we knew at a young age now seems folly, misguided and naive. What could I know of parenting before I became a parent? Likewise, of the people I would met, countries visit, food taste and sounds heard etc. all have expanded my understanding in the ever-changing world.

I have come to realize that life comprises only two days: a day for you and a day against you. When it favours you, don't be reckless, when there are challenges have patience as your guiding virtue; both days will expire! As such, if you can't be a bridge to connect people, don't be a wall to separate them. If you can't be a light to brighten people's good deeds, don't be darkness covering their efforts. If you can't be water to help people's crops sprout, don't be a pest destroying them. If you can't be a vaccine to give life, don't be a virus to terminate it. If you can't be a pencil to write someone's happiness, be nice and try to erase their sadness. You are not someone's keeper but you can be their pillar of hope. Cheers!

As for God and the afterlife, that isn't for me. I'm all for faith (though don't have any) less so organised religion. I respect (if not agree) with all unique beliefs and perspectives. For example, why is there such a despicable concept as original sin? I can't abide the, do this don't do that mantra. It's only through mistakes that we learn; we shouldn't be castigated for them. All I know, shit sometimes happens.

The walk of life is certainly not always easy; it entails both joys and challenges. If we are fortunate one will find love and purpose. This poem collection explores the profound experiences in the circle of life, from birth to death the cradle to the grave. What it means to be a child and parent sometimes simultaneously. How one faces insurmountable obstacles and finds ways to overcome them. That the most important lesson, is, to understand oneself and one's place in the world. Life truly is about embracing the journey more than reaching the final destination. As such, I advocate acknowledging that life is unpredictable and that failure is an inherent part of the human experience. To differentiate between wrong decisions and poor results. That it is fine, healthy even to reward yourself for good decisions even if it ends in a bad outcome. I call this mind-set, being a life pirate. It is an attitude that encourages us to live with purpose and authenticity, accepting that the journey may not always unfold as expected. By being a life pirate, we seize the opportunities that come our way, treasure the lessons learned from our failures, and navigate the ever-changing seas of life with courage and resilience.

LIFE'S JOURNEY

Life is a journey filled with endless possibilities. Who you meet, how you live, what adventures you have, where you visit, what work you do, what will be the highs and lows and so on. At the start of any given day, you can't predict how it will finish. Will it continue on as expected or be the start of the next stage of your life? These are sliding-door moments, watersheds. Will you move forward with someone or once more be by yourself? Will alcohol, sex and friends feature in smaller quantities as a de-facto crutch in life or one can manage without them as you understand and become more comfortable with your true self?

Should I fear death and getting older, embrace it or fight for every second? If I go kicking and screaming, how painful will that process be? I'm not scared of the physical distress, but the emotional strain I'll cause my loved ones may be too much to bear. I must ask, how can I make the most of what time I have left? How do I focus on what is most meaningful? Can I reconcile with those I have bad blood with and, treasure those precious moments with family and friends? I should make up my mind on the God question.

Death is central to the human condition even if it's so rarely talked about in certain cultures. I have so many questions yet few answers. Should I be afraid or accepting of the inevitable? If I know I'm going to die, is this better than ignorance of the when and how or will it or add unnecessary burden? I have come to the conclusion, that there can be no life without death. I must use my remaining months, years or hopefully decades, to really enjoy the preciousness of life and savour each moment. It's living authentically that we can truly make the most of our time on this earth.

What is the Essence of Life?

We were born and we will die.
We will go from the cradle to the grave.
From whence we came, we will surely go;
this a singular truth we all know.
It's the journey and not the destination that's the essence of life.

To live is to experience.
To swim like a fish or fly like an eagle.
To wonder and explore.
To laugh and cry.
To hear tales and be part of stories.

To be proud but suffer from pride.
To cherish and to throw away.
To regret and to have joy.
To be sick and to be strong.
To lift heavy burdens or not have a care in the world.

To love and to be loved.
To hurt and to be hurt.
To be alone but not lonely.
To cry tears of joy and sadness.
To have passion for what you love and be passionate with the ones you love.

To have animal instincts but a human heart.
To find a partner or be single.
To have parents and be a parent.
To believe or be an unbeliever.
To be a dreamer but with a rational brain.

To have all that you wanted but still want more.
To think the grass is greener on the other side.
To want your cake and eat it.
To fight wars with yourself and with others,
to find peace with others and within yourself.

This is what it means to "live your days."
Unending questions with no right answers.
This is why you're unique,
why there's only one you.

Others will know who you are but only you truly know yourself!
This is the essence of life and what it means to be alive.

Watershed

Watersheds,
sliding-door moments,
those times in life,
few but vital,
important,
life-changing,
inputting,
defining,
decision-making
often difficult choosing.

Go with heart or brain when getting married or divorced?
What makes you serve in the forces or emergency services?
How will life change when your become a parent?

These are watershed moments,
life-defining choices,
a mental leap from before to after,
where you knew what the world had to offer,
how it spun,
to a time of space walking,
contemplating,
new exploring,
mind combobulating,
stretching,
possibly breaking.

These are times when decisions unsure,
outcomes unknown.
Sliding-door moments,

the before and after on your life journey,
one emotion at the time from cradle to grave.

That point in time,
a gut feeling that life will go one way or other,
left, right or forward,
certainly not backwards.

At these watershed moments,
don't be reactive,
better proactive.
Make the decision,
weigh the consequences,
the pros and cons,
the probabilities versus potentials,
all the unknowns,
the...
this is the correct option at this point and time
no matter the fuck-ups that might come with it.

Be strong in conviction,
this half the battle,
the brain too much rattle when overthink,
analyse,
leading to paralysis,
no decision-taking,
keep sleep-walking-
talking the talk not walking the walk.

Don't be afraid of consequences,
know how to mitigate,
reduce the emotional fluctuate,
not let life stagnate,
put balls in hand and anticipate,
get ready to accelerate,
screw regurgitate,
don't think propagate,
but overtake,
consolidate and partner create,
enough contemplate,
no more stagnation,
time for regeneration.

Don't be afraid of watershed moments!

Disability

I'm a lucky bugger,
never bad illness or serious crash,
born with a body all in good working order,
a mind that sorts out shit,
no complaints this end nor natural gifts.

Yeah,
I would change a few things,
a bit of extra height,
faster mataboliam,
but this cosmetic…
I've been a lucky bugger.

Inspiration,
I, meeting a hero,
not for them managing their quadriplegia,
road accident at 17,
but for all they have to give-
leader of band,
singer,
theatre impessinario,
helping me to raise charity funds,
their interaction,
the greatest gift.
Another friend,
of being born handicapped,
but that not handicapping him,
as he does most interesting work,
meet princesses,
survive tsunamis,
terrorist attack,
their life one of marvel,
not just survival but thrival,
truly exceptional.

Disability a fact,
not defining,
they refining,
finding a way to still leading,
mental invigorating,
spiritual building,
I contemplating,
revering.

I with my natural born luck that might change tomorrow,
might be taken just like that,
seeing those who inspire,
that no mountain is too high,
who understand the true meaning of sisu.

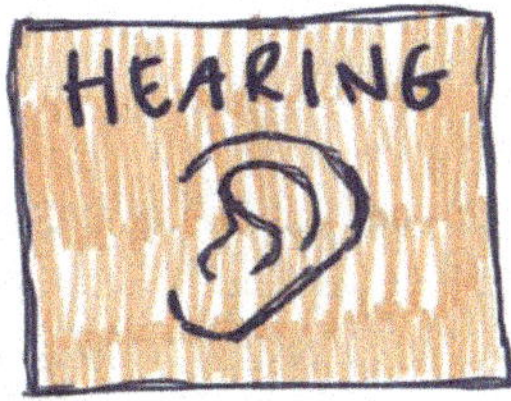

4-in-1

I'm 4-in-1 so don't label me;
I'm neither more nor less than the sum of my parts.

I'm a businessman…
that loves the thrill of the chase,
a contract,
a client,
the working as part of a team or hailing personal glory,
of finding mental strength,
perseverance when things don't go my way.

I'm 4-in-1 so don't label me;
I'm neither more nor less than the sum of my parts.

I'm a creative man…
who sees beauty in the ordinary,
extravagance in the mundane.
I love the challenge of telling a story from a new perspective,
the psychological gymnastics to overcome doubts,
rejection from the majority when seeing the world through a different lens.

I'm 4-in-1 so don't label me;
I'm neither more nor less than the sum of my parts.

I'm a crazy man…
who will do what whim decides,
the devil visiting my right shoulder
kicking the ass of the angel on my right.
I will do what I know is wrong or stupid,
this is the, no rules, me,
the, not give a damn, me,
the me who will take risks not calculated,
who goes with gut or serendipity over logic,
who revels in the unknown and outrageous.

I'm 4-in-1 so don't label me;
I'm neither more nor less than my whole.

I have to wear many hats to live my life.
I'm a family man…
the future of my children is the reason why I try business.
I'm creative to get through the stresses of life,
to find solutions to insurmountable problems;
I need crazy times to keep a sense of self.

I'm 4-in-1 so don't label me;
I'm neither more nor less than the sum of my parts.

Life Odyssey

Where is my life going?
Nowhere fast...
like my hospitalised dad.
Work is slowly strangling me,
lawyers are fucking with me,
my marriage disintegrating.

I have to get out into the world,
see hope in summer skies,
in the people I pass,
anyone or anything which might change my life for the better,
it can't get worse.

I leave the front door,
turn left and start my odyssey.
It's grey and drizzling,
this as it's been the whole week,
this,
the perfect analogy to my mood,
my emotions,
my current life.

I'm cheered by the muezzin calling the faithful to prayer.
I'm reminded,
there was life before mine as there will be for centuries after.

I walk past the tram stop,
my breath this time not creating a fog on a cold day,
this though how I feel it should.

Five miles pass,
I'm still stuck in my mind.
The zip on my jeans now broken…
as is my mental state,
my soul and boxers barely covered.

Though I have no destination I change my direction of travel.
Where I was going had no end,
no reason.
I will let whim control if I go left or right,
where I stop for food or alcoholic beverage,
what I do next today and in life.

I sit in a park,
chat with friends on WhatsApp,
hear stories and share jokes,
but what I want,
need is company and not via digital means.

I desire a smile to light up my heart,
words that can sing to my soul,
memories to be made,
maybe bodies shared?

I stop,
eat,
lunch filling my stomach
but not my heart;
I need something to kick start my day,
re-energize my life.

I leave the cafe and continue on hoping fate will intervene.

I see kiosk upon boutique,
but I'm not one for retail therapy.
I keep walking,
wandering,
mind pondering,
wondering...

I pass sex shops and kinos,
DildoKing adverts abound…
truly,
his majesty!

It's been a while since I've been between a women's legs...
and when I say, a while...

just for clarification,
not obfuscation,
I'm talking days and weeks,
not months and years;
everything relative as I tell my truth,
reveal my life.

I pass a sex shop,
a dozen in less than half-a-mile.

I see purple vibrators,
bondage gear,
crotchless panties and gimp suits;
my mind is cartwheeling.

I think of women of yesteryear,
open-minded and body mounted,
each with their different limit,
how much they push me and I them.

The quiet one who liked biting.
The noisy one…
who was just noise.
The Asian girl,
quite the thrill.
Arab,
she hated me;
it was complicated.
The black woman,
six times cumming in her sack.
The last white,
belly a frightful sight,
but ass so tight.

God damn!
Passing the sex shop,
joys and disappointment relived.
Kino next door,
woman on tap,
give me a slap,
wake me from memories and fantasies,
let me continue on,
straight ahead...
not thinking about getting head.

I turn around,
I do go into the shop selling sex,
I don't know why?
Why do I frustrate myself,
mentally castrate myself as I see a world,
experiences out of reach?

My truth,
I have no girl to share a laugh or bed with;
I've forgotten what a warm body feels like.

My frustrations are building.
I want cum gurgling,
pussy squirting,
but this is pure fantasizing,
not life living,
body joining,
soul uniting,
more like self-destructing.

I am human,
happy in my own company but need more than self.
I have jealousy of seeing others enjoy,
excite,
delight,
reunite in another's presence;
this is nearly finishing,
killing me.

I'm not happy with my status quo.
having to compromise as there's no solution,
conclusion to marriage explosion.

I'm kidding myself hoping for change,
to break the stick,
finding someone or something significant,
not be contained,
constrained;
this is a mad way to live,
survival not thrival,
not living to my limit,
excelling as I should,
but living in a mental shoe box,
hell,
this, the antithesis of living.

Fuck this shit!
I'll find a way out of mental prison,
do what I need.

I want relaxation and attention,
to let my mind float away,
troubles left for another day.

I see a sign offering a massage,
I don't want a happy ending,
just forgetfulness.

I enter.

The sauna burns away my miseries,
the masseuse pushes away my worries,
the steam-room helps me let go of anger.

I return to the world one hour later,
refreshed and reinvigorated,
not ready to take on the world as in days of old,
but vigour returned.

I stop in a bar to contemplate life,
the sun gliding across the sky as the first froth of a beer touches my lips.

I know life will end,
mine as much as my dad's,
so must make the most of my days,
spend time with my kids while they're still young,
find fulfilment in my work and make love to a woman who wants me;
there is no other way to life odyssey.

Decade in the Sun

I know the past
and live a present;
predicting the future…
a fool's game.

Where will my life be in 10 years when 10 days
can seem like infinity,
10 seconds feeling like an hour?

God willing,
though I'm doubting,
Earth spinning,
I'll still be alive.

Will I be married and have started a new family
or living a singleton life?
Will women and beer still be my soulmates,
my addictions in equal measure and pleasure?

Over the next decade,
will my life be one of peace or dramatics?
Will I become president and transformed by
bionic limbs,
or a homeless,
penniless drunk?

Will I experience great heights or be brought to
my knees?
Will I live in a castle or tent?
How often will I be devastated and elevated?

In a decade's time…
will I be six feet under,
a box in the soil my final resting place,
or 5 million metres up…
in the stars…
on a spaceship?

What will life be like in the wider world?
How will this chaotic earth that's tilting on its
technological,
political,
economical and climatic axis be moving?
Will intelligence be artificial or real?
Will reality be virtual or augmented?
Will we exist in this dimension or the sixth?

Death or space,
I can't predict.
The joy of the unknown,
of living the journey and not worrying about the
destination,
of embracing uncertainty,
is the defining characteristic of being human,
of feeling alive,
of being a life pirate.

Ten years,
a decade of decisions and consequences,
of success and failures,
this is life rollercoaster.

The Queen's Speech?

I'm eight,
my days are innocent and the new year coming.
I don't know what the morning will bring,
what surprises lie in stockings,
what joy and heartache I will experience before the day is out.

Last night I wrote Santa a letter,
put cookies and milk under the tree.
Today, my father wears a red suit and bushy beard,
we listen to the Queen's speech and watch Dalton play Bond;
this, my last Crimbo as a child.

Turn of the millennium,
a yuletide haze,
booze and pills fog self-hate;
I want answers,
I want peace,
I want to end my life.

Middle-age,
my kids,
my joys,
my life are in Christmases left behind.

Where once the future was full of possibilities...
there is now no more sandcastle boy or dancing girl.

A past of Christmas disappointments,
questions and hurt,
but I have hope for future festivities of love and hope.

Christmas,
many look forward for months,
others, don't like being reminded of advancing years and sad memories.

I worry history will repeat,
that I'll make the same mistakes and drive those closest away,
that I'll have Christmas pudding and brandy butter for one,
nobody to share my life journey with.

The Week

Next week like no other:
Tuesday dad's funeral,
Wednesday spread the ashes,
Thursday start divorce,
Friday having HIV test.

My dad,
45 years of being the rock of my life
his family,
the cool head when others lost theirs,
the emotional and financial stability no more,
he, now out of pain,
glad now resting;
my world spinning on its axis.

Next week like no other:
Tuesday dad's funeral,
Wednesday spread the ashes,
Thursday start divorce,
Friday having HIV test.

The ashes will return,
this man,
soon to be in the wind,
scattered next to cricket pitch and Officers Mess;
it's a mind-fuck,
reminded of own mortality;
my world spinning on its axis.

Next week like no other:
Tuesday dad's funeral,
Wednesday spread the ashes,
Thursday start divorce,
Friday having HIV test.

Knowing only one life,
that should lead happy as my father did,
the time is now for new starts,
to break from my past,
build a new future with my kids,
start a fresh life and hopefully love;
my world spinning on its axis.

Next week like no other:
Tuesday dad's funeral,
Wednesday spread the ashes,
Thursday start divorce,
Friday having HIV test.

I have to go forward confidently,
know my status,
see if my philandering has caught up with me or
I have missed that bullet,
my need for emotional,
sexual connection these last years,
overwhelming my desire to keep being the rock
for my family;
my world spinning on its axis.

Next week like no
other:
Tuesday dad's
funeral,
Wednesday spread
the ashes,
Thursday start
divorce,
Friday having HIV
test.

How next week
goes,
only god knows,
i having to remain
stoical,
no matter my emotions,
my world shortly to be spinning on its axis.

Next week is like no other:
Tuesday dad's funeral,
Wednesday spread the ashes,
Thursday start divorce,
Friday having HIV test.

WHAT A YEAR THIS WEEK HAS BEEN

Shoes- Part 1

I am office shoes.
I am loafers with no socks.
I am transparent plastic sandals.
I am white retro trainers.
I am army boots.
I am Dr Martin's.
I am walking shoes.
I am high heels.
I have fat gold chains on my footwear.
Sports trainers I'm in.
Knee high kinky boots for me…
but who am I other than a fellow life passenger?

Do you think you know me?
Why your prejudices concerning my footwear?

Am I an office worker?
Mother?
Punk?
Immigrant?
Pub owner?
Student?
Entrepreneur?
Civil servant?

Can you match the shoes to me?

Maybe you think you can,
but my shoes don't define who I am;
it's self-expression like my clothes,
my haircut,
visible ink and metal adornments.

Stare if you want,
come to wrong conclusions;
know this:
I'm living my reality,
100% organic not fake news.

Shoes- Part 2

Shoes,
I'm tip taping on the dance floor,
you are taking me towards an angel.

Shoes,
my heart broken and mind destroyed,
you walking me back to love.

Shoes,
you are my wings,
you carry me to the marriage altar.

Shoes,
we are hiking up a mountain,
to swim in a lake and make love in a tent.

Shoes,
I feel your tiny soles on my back,
my essence for being complete.

Shoes,
you are my companion,
to all that is good.

Shoes,
we walk round a corner and see my wife talking animatedly.

Shoes,
you are witness to arguments,
plates being thrown.

Shoes,
you take me upstairs to an empty bed.

Shoes,
we are in the kitchen,
another evening of cooking for one.

Shoes,
you took me through the front door,
leaving me with broken heart.

Shoes,
we go to the pub where you will help me drown my sorrows.

Shoes,
we are going feet first down the church aisle.

Gangsters

Having a walk,
having a laugh,
a think,
a drink,
minding my business.

Enter a bar,
not far on my journey from A to C,
quite the what or will be,
who knows,
I just need magic sauce,
some fizz and a whizz,
a pint not cocktail,
no mocktail,
sparkling water or baby sham for me,
I need a man's drink,
not top shelf kitchen sink,
gay twink,
I, a man not a boy,
toy,
can't be pushed around physically,
emotionally,
mentally-
no one will fuck with me.

Go for a sit,
have a slip,
beer on a blazer,
dangerous eyes glare,
I'm in deep shit!

Arm behind back,
Spanish Inquisition rack,
frogmarched into room,
if I could,
I would shit out my sack.

Smiley teeth,
bristly face,
slapped round chops,
kick to the ass and thrown out.

Fresh air tasting nectar,
I living another day,
one more life episode.

Go back into the night with no fear
scared shitless by gangsters,
lucky it didn't end, oh dear!

Accountabilities

Decisions are not easy,
that is why you have to decide,
to come to a conclusion,
to do what you think has the best overall outcome.

There will never be a 100% right decision,
life, chess not chequers,
unending choices;
it's an art not science.

Forward or back?
Married or single?
God or heathen?
Children or childless?
Responsibility or freedom?
Accountability or doing what your heart desires?
Car or bike?
Vegan or pig?
Divorced or stay miserable?
Life…or the life less ordinary?
Girls or boys?
Positive or negative?
Feeling sorry for yourself or being pro-active?
Clarity or a mind like a thousand frogs?
Terrestrial or digital?
Living life in monochrome or rainbow colours?
Tram or tube?
Sensible or reckless?
What is expected of you... or decide your destiny?
Dog or cat?
Black or white?
Gay or straight?
Trying to have it all or settling for mediocre?
Life thriller or boring filler?
Killer or peacemaker?
Tears of joy or those of a clown?
Security or aim for the moon?
A free bird or caged parrot?

There is no correct answer in life,
just choices with outcomes,
some good others less so.

This is what it means to be human,
to be an adult,
to make decisions,
be responsible for the impact,
accountable for choices.

So, do not prevaricate,
obfuscate or other long words that mean procrastinate!
Know, there will be positive and negative consequences to your choices,
your conclusions.

Whether left or right,
up or down,
stay or go,
choose carefully and own your decision,
accept your responsibilities.

The Week

Monday

Life,
love,
work,
nothing going to plan...
or is that the plan?

Fate,
brace not hate,
have to decipher and try make sense,
no idea what will be hence,
what tomorrow will bring,
if the sun will rise,
the stars sparkle;
my future in the hand of the gods.

Good vibes on that,
bad news on this,
my life a constant rollercoaster.

I need a partner to ride or die with,
another life pirate on the sea of uncertainty,
be certain in the unknown.
comfortable being uncomfortable,
who can take each day as an adventure,
something to savour,
explore,
not bore.

Who considers life is never enough,
always wanting more,
the next challenge to overcome,
opportunity taken,
success and failures,
multiple possibilities,
realities,
all on the whim of maybes.

Tuesday

My gut instinct told me,
it's not right,
she not someone I want to hang with...
but life,
been a bit lonely,
what's the worst that can happen?

She's a high class woman,
who like high class lounges,
with high priced drinks.

I don't mind high or
low class girls,
where go or what drink,
it's the company that
matters not the
environment,
not, the having to be
seen in classy places.

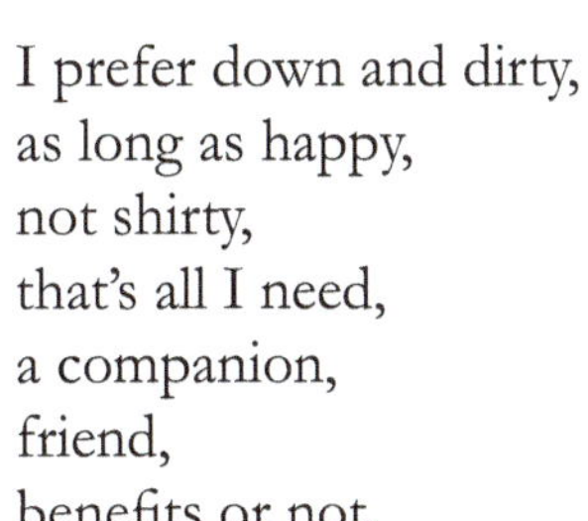

I prefer down and dirty,
as long as happy,
not shirty,
that's all I need,
a companion,
friend,
benefits or not.

Like me or don't,
I'm good either way as long as your genuine,
living free and being honest.

We go from A to B,
taxi girl making more than fair margin.

That her job,
income,
feel like I'm being screwed…
not in a good way,
reasonable way;
this not humanity,
but bestiality.

New place,
new drink,
go to toilet,
come back cocktails lined up.
Not my flavour but will go with it.
6 shots, I'm told,
price to go with it;
only taste one,
been drinking too many years.

This not right,
taken advantage of,
I'm no mugg.

Bar staff think I'm a cunt,
that I won't make a fuss in front of lovely lady,
that I'm a rich foreigner;
wrong person,
Bitch!

They compound,
fuck up the bill.
This ridiculous,
this life,
this is a bar will not go again,
this,
time for bed,
this, makes me miss my Captain Morgan girl,
my fellow Konyagi ambassador.

Wednesday

I only have one life,
what to do?
Get back on the horse,
of course.
I must keep living life and go back into the emotional battlefield of ups, downs and unknowns.

Agree to meet someone random,
don't know what to expect,
hopefully a bit more respect.

We chat,
we drink,
bit of a laugh,
she full of interesting facts.
Where does the word kangaroo come from?
Aborigine for, I don't know!
Flag colours and Alsatian origins?
Who knows this shit?

She nice but not wow.
Go back to mine,
she juicy boobies,
tiny nips,
bit of belly,
narrow hips.

A person who can be a friend,
this a welcome night,
this why I love life,
everybody different,
everybody a story to tell,
I just need a person to listen,
explore,
open mind and heart to head.

Thursday

What a shit day,
it all gone pants,
a skid stain on my life,
worse than the trouble and strife.

Hopes dashed,
plans have to be forgotten,
life gone rotten,
my soul crushed,
have to start again,
pull on my resilience,
it's not brilliance,
just acceptance of the pros and cons,
of being a life pirate.

Friday

I only have one life,
what to do?
Get back on the horse,
of course.

Must live it,
back into the emotional battlefield of ups, downs
and unknowns.
Back into the night,
not knowing,
not caring what will happen,
but have to move forward,
be proactive,
make shit happen as who knows what the tide
will bring in!

Map of My Life

Tattoos,
got a few,
maybe more to come,
these, the map of my life.

I share my experience,
my life,
who I am and what I represent to all who see my tattoos.

My soul,
beliefs,
passions,
my humanity exposed for the world to see,
my loves symbolised,
iconography of who I am and what I represent to those who see my tattoos.

The right arm,
family.
Chinese soulmate,
14 years together coming to an end.
The 4 bees,
my 4 Bs,
4 kids.
The Arabic,
meaning, this is life,
the Bs my life.

Tattoos,
got a few,
maybe more to come,
these, the map of my life.

The left arm,
me,
the individual the who lives temet nosce,
true to himself.

I use meraki to remind me of passion for creativity,
sisu, that I'm indomitable,
ikigai is all that makes me,
good and bad,
happy and sad.

Tattoos,
got a few,
maybe more to come,
these, the map of my life.

On my back,
a free bird for this is who I am.
Below,
ying and yang,
pulled between family and individual,
trying to find unity,
this my reality,
currently disharmony,
confusion.

Family vs individual,
the internal struggle,
fight.
Altruistic or selfish?
There is no in-between,
no being both.

Parenting,
marriage,
the ultimate compromise of life.
Trying to get through,
day at a time working it out,
how to satisfy all,
dodge the grenade,
wear an emotional flak jacket.

Tattoos,
got a few,
maybe more to come,
these, the map of my life.

Soon,
one more to add,
Epictetus quote:
Circumstances don't make the man,
they only reveal him to himself.
this, as I know of challenges to come.

New Beginnings

The last 12 months all doom and gloom,
fuck that shit,
new country,
continent,
going to soon.

It's a start over and new choices,
can't know how it'll play out,
workout,
precious life,
continual marriage fallout,
new life,
hopefully rejoices.

Foreign fields soon to tread,
I go hopeful heart,
soon depart,
make things happen,
If don't do that,
scared of failure,
who am I?
Life would be whole lot paler,
all have to say,
screw you, dread.

New friends to be found,
experiences had,
this what I live for,
helps to bury the sad.

The past will always be there,
choices and decisions sometimes scare,
but end of the day,
do what I must,
in living life,
this my hundred percent trust.

Only one life,
we all must live,
be true to self,
this the biggest give.

Don't be shy,
always ask why,
but be that mother-fucker,
aim for the sky.

Might not hit the moon,
but don't stop trying,
when you lose hope,
you start dying.

So hit the stars,
as that who you are,
you and me,
we not commuter car.

No matter the ups and downs,
this just life,
remember yourself,

not the ex-wife.

I'll mental journey with you forever,
that's a promise,
we, together.

Don't believe there's a single person ride and die,
but how through understanding, love and support,
friends can eat from the same pie.

What tomorrow will bring,
who can know,
but tonight, I know,
karaoke I'll go.

I'll sing like Aretha and dance like a dervish,
there's no other choice,
but to live life fullish.

So, this is my ode,
to new starts beginning,
remember and love for my kids,
the shit in my life…
I'll be binning!

Inner Wolf

You thought I was a lovely Labrador,
compliant,
pliable,
daft,
liked chasing a tennis ball into muddy pond,
that you were my mistress,
could boss me...
but you never saw self-control,
my inner wolf,
cold hearted decision-maker,
rule breaker…
but today, that all changes,
fangs you will see!

I will be the one making you come to heel,
if you don't,
soon you will squeal,
your strategy as useless as a banana peel,
you the one slipping on it!
my job now,
help the kids emotionally feel my love,
heal.

You took for granted all I did for you,
for the children,
not the resolve needed to always implement,
I needed heart of pure cement,
be unbreakable…
so I could look after you,
but, today, you will feel the heat,
the fear of facing,
confronting my inner wolf,
the demon that I've shielded,
hid from you because I loved you,
you who used and abused,
tried to confuse with lies and manipulation.
You who has taken kids from me,
Tried to turn those I love against me,
but they had trust in me,
our bonds of family or friendship,
unbreakable,
as to, that of my children,

I believe they will also,
in time,
see who I really am,
who you really are,
the daughter that never wanted to be her mother.

May the kids forgive you for all your putting
them through,
as, whereas I'm adult,
can take slings and arrows,
stones hurting more than words,
understanding this all part of life,
trouble and strife,
angry ex-wife,
they are innocent souks that you've corrupted,
manipulated,
mind combobulated and that's unforgiveable.

And so, today, it changes,
no more backfoot defence and manning the mental barricades,
rather,
I will go on attack,
offence.

I've given you enough rope…
and now will pull it tight,

give you a helluva fright,
the noose tightening,
going taut on your lies,
your only hope,
back down,
admit the truth...
it will set you free.

Today you will see my inner wolf,
the leader of the pack who others follow,
believe in,
not because of the noise I make,
but actions take and fearlessness show.

The truth…
you are,
always were just a pack member,
not the general you think,
claim.
You rose high on my shoulders,
I letting you have your moment,
but now it's time to put you back in place,
not because I'm vindictive,
but you have pushed me too hard for too long,
think, I'm not mentally strong…
the truth,
I was too unrestrictive,
love obsessive,
you taking advantage of this,
thinking your someone more than you are,
now,
it's time to close the lid on that jam jar.

Hibernation

With the whirlwind raging,
I was emotional hibernating,
defence pose from incoming blows and kicks,
plastic chairs and chains on handbags,
not soft sticks.

I was taking cover from the physical as much as mental,
emotional,
financial,
loss of love special,
but now no more sleep,
time to get proactive life repeat,
as I'm tired of lies,
out of hibernation I'll come…
and I'm hungry,
very fucking angry,
the bear in me reappearing,
soon dominating,
making life what I wish,
not here to give hatred a cold dish,
the truth more devastating,
this my salvation,
redemption,
I'm tired of too much contemplation,
star gaze constellation,
now time for action.

I will kick down doors,
lead meetings,
take back the control that was taken from me,
my children that were taken from me,
my life taken from me,
soon you will be hiding from the whirlwind,
I no longer hibernating,
but been reinvigorating,
this, you better be believing!

Keep On Keeping On

A tough day,
tough week,
tough life.

I do my best,
leave nothing on the table,
give it my all;
there is no training manual,
no best practice approach how to live.

Take day at a time,
know, I will reach highs and be crushed by lows.
There will be success and failure,
challenges and opportunities;
on any given timeline
I will be pawn or king.

This is the laundry of life,
the spin-dryer of experience,
and so there is only one way to live,
your way!

Be honest to yourself,
live your truth,
find your motivation,
love family and keep friends.

I say,
I will not fade,
go quiet into the darkness,
but fight till the last,
till I have walked up the shadow of the valley of
death...
I,
will,
always keep on keeping on,
be me and live temet nosce.

WE ARE BORN ALONE

From baby to child to teenager to adult to parent and maybe grandparent, the passing of generations unfolds before our eyes. My kids are everything… as I expect I was for my parents. Being a proud parent is my reason for getting up in the morning. They provide a sense of purpose as I push myself to work even when I have no love for what I do, a complete lack of personal fulfilment.

Being a parent is one of the few things in life that the division between the have and have nots is black and white. There is no in-between or shades of grey. No sliding-scale such as rich to poor. You're either a parent or you're not! It's a role that encompasses immense responsibility and selflessness. As parents, we give our all, dedicate ourselves to the well-being and happiness of our children. In return, we may not receive tangible rewards but are blessed with the unconditional trust that parenthood brings. Parenting is a testament to the ultimate form of altruism, where we invest ourselves completely knowing that the true reward lies in the love we share with our children

These poems delve into the intricacies of parenting, capturing the moments of joy, the worries that keep us awake at night, and the profound sense of fulfilment that comes from nurturing and guiding another human being. If you too are a father. I'm sure you have an idea how I'm feeling.

Every Sperm is Sacred

One sperm fertilises an egg,
a shot at infancy,
a billion sparks of energy,
two becoming one.

The first signs of pregnancy,
unexpected vomiting,
crazy-eating then water-breaking,
this, the starting of a new life journeying,
rollercoastering.

I know what to expect,
I've experienced it twice before with my shorty.
We have new hope in our hearts,
a baby once again centre of our lives,
defining who we are.

This is an extra chance to care for someone more than myself,
to mould a new life,
for that is what it means to be a father;
let me not fail him or her.

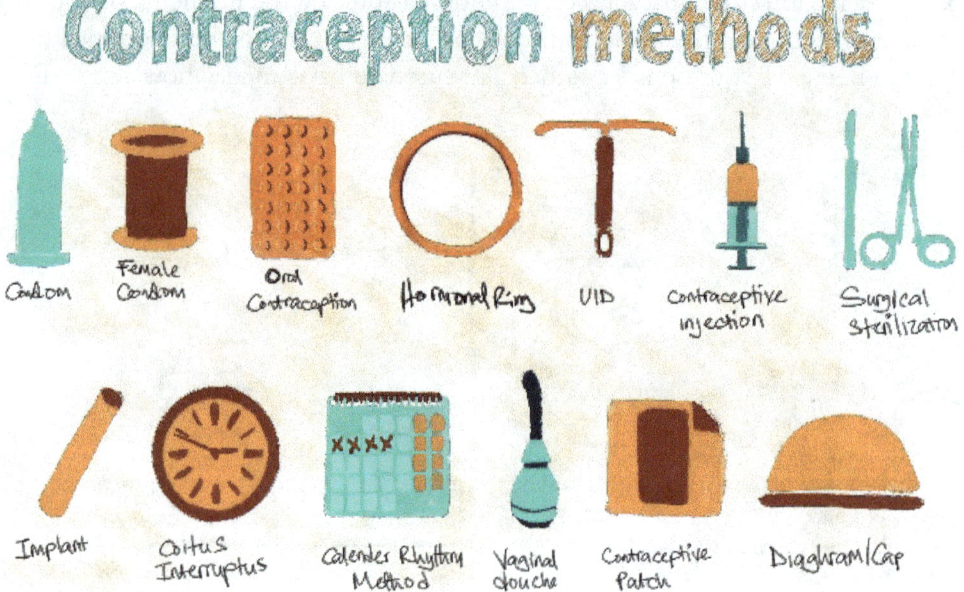

Fatherhood

I sit nervously in the waiting-room…
will I hear wails of life or death?
Shed tears of thanks or despair?
I pray for baby screams as I sit nervously in the waiting-room.

I sit nervously in the waiting-room…
not knowing if I will be a good father to my son.

I try to remember lessons learnt from my pa,
learning from his successes and failures,
those too of granddad.

From my seed life lives in fleshy folds.
A face like mine but more rounded.
Ears mine,
lips hers.

Toes mine,
fingers hers,
chin granddad's.

My son,
his senses alert,
knows who and what they can trust.
The reassuring face, smell, voice, touch;
they can feel the love implicit between father and son.

When I see pictures of me as a baby,
I see the love my father had for me,
the care he showed,
the responsibility that sat on his shoulder for his son,
his forever sandcastle boy.

That bond between father and son is unique, special.
The senior leading by example,
loving, teaching and grooming their son to be a father one day.

When I was a child,
I spoke, thought and reasoned as a child,
but when I grew up,
I put away childish thoughts.
As a father,
I better understand this circle of life,
the passing of generations from baby to boy to man to grandfather.
That my little bundle of joy will soon be an adult,
the centre of his own triumphs and calamities.

Our generations are markedly different.
The opportunities and challenges I faced were not the same as those of my father,
nor will my boy's experience be that of his dad,
but, I will always be there for him,
helping to crest waves and survive tragedies.

What will happen through his days,
I don't, can't know.
Will he get into trouble with the police,
play truant,
break windows,
get drunk,
shoplift,
smoke dope…
as were my teenage rebellions?

How can I be his voice of reason?
What can I tell him about what he should or shouldn't do?
Which of my life lessons will I share as he transitions from child, through puberty and into adulthood?

What sort of a father will I be as he enters a world in turmoil and my universe of chaos?
The responsibility for his young life sits on my shoulders;
I must be his rock,
his constant,
his point of manly reference.

There are no pass marks for being a dad,
but I hope,
one day,
he will make me a proud grandparent,
and say:
I want to be the father to my children as you were to me.

Daughters

I, a girl,
a daughter,
soon to be woman,
mother.

My mum,
my role model,
my teacher in a house of boys.

I watch and observe,
follow and imitate,
do as she does and act like she is.

Our parents are our teachers,
we are nature and nurture,
every boy will grow into a version of their father,
daughters their mothers;
this, is the circle of life.

Double Trouble

I have a boy,
but my daughters have a special corner of my heart.

I see my little girls,
my life,
in the form of her mother,
my sweet love miniaturised.

Their innocence will go as they morph into women.
They will not always small,
I can't cocoon them forever,
that's not the circle of life.

I hope they don't suffer the way I made women suffer.
I pray they can be strong like their mum,
their role model.

I will try to protect them from men like me,
who want their way and have cheap thrills but
don't consider the consequences.
I must instruct her brother to be a better man than me,
to respect women and look out for his sisters.

I will try to give wisdom,
teach my girls the lessons I've learned.

I hope they will live their lives
loud and proud,
that they will be confident in all they do.

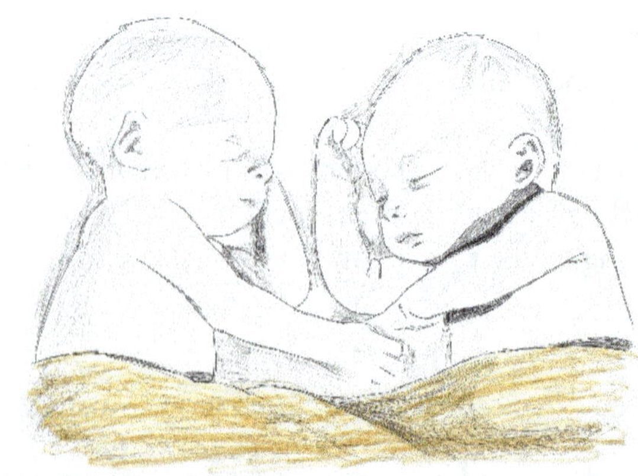

A Different Friday Night

It's Friday,
my favourite time of the week,
but tonight I'm not with mates….
I'm on dad duty.

Little sproglet in arms,
I, a bottle of milk in hands,
shitty nappies and puke my new best friends.

My love is up town,
having a night on the tiles;
I couldn't be happier for her,
for us.

My Reason for Living

I can't put into words what I feel for you;
you will only know this if you too have a child.

Your vulnerability, my ultimate responsibility!
Your life, literally in my hands.
You will follow what I tell you;
my word,
your gospel.

I'm here to protect you,
to help you grow into adulthood.

I pray your will be happier,
more confident,
more successful than me;
I will do anything to make your dreams come true.

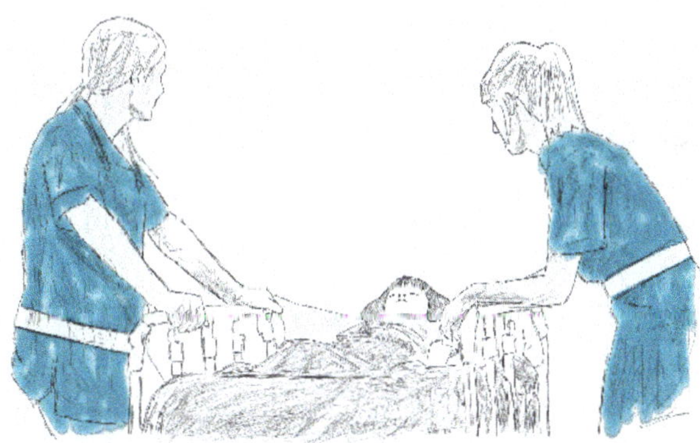

I try to lead by example but have many foibles and faults.
I will sometimes fail you,
I will make mistakes,
and that's, ok–
failure is also a life lesson in growing-up;
the important point,
be accountable for your actions.

Life is full of ups and downs,
good and bad,
this is what it means to be human.
You will experience highs and lows,
continually ride the waves and rolling hills of your reality;
I only hope you will find your way,
your path to happiness.

Know this:
there's no pain like the pain I feel when you're in pain.

The pain of your broken arm,
a cut heart,
a wounded soul.

Pain comes in many guises and I would gladly take yours,
I would take all your pain,
buy it at any cost;
through your pain see my love for you.

I pray that you'll be happier,
more confident,
more successful than me;
I will do everything in my power to make your dreams come true,
but I won't promise what I can't deliver.

I hope one day I will become a proud grandparent,
you learning of parenting from my success and failures of being a parent.

I love you.

Three Ages of Abandonment

Kindergarten

Warm bed to cold floor.
Pyjamas to uniform.
Freedom to rules.
Mum to teachers.
Known to unsure.
Boobs to packed lunch.
Why?
WHY?
WHY DID YOU ABONDON ME?!?

Father

My father,
my hero,
his words my command.
My actions,
to please him.
My actions,
to rebel,
to be my own man,
to leave his shadow,
to one day have my own family,
to be a father.
To not make his mistakes but my own.
To live my life with his guidance but not in his shoes.
He is human,
he was my god,
he abandoned me.

Boarding School

I leave,
packed off;
I'm not sure why.

New bed,
new food,
wash clothes,
clean floors.

Discipline and a regimental clock my present and future.
Be here now,
do this then,

prefects like parents
teachers are gods.

I'm told:
this is for your own good,
to learn to stand up for yourself.
That, it's preparation to enter the adult world…
but I'm still a child;
why have I been abandoned a third time?

4 Bs

Brooklyn

From small boy to big man,
I've always been there for you,
loved you,
done everything for you,
you, everything a dad should be proud of,
doing well for yourself,
for your young siblings despite all the chaos.

Just know,
as from the first time,
for all time,
be free with me,
live you as you,
I, only want what's best for you,
simple!

Barney

I die and cry for what taken away,
you my first born,
see so much of myself in you,
wanting to please,
prove yourself for love…
know, I will always be there for you,
these just difficult times,
lying crimes,
heart broken,
sad rhythms,
don't know what to do so you know I love you,
insane legal lines,
but you my boy,
golf shooting stick,
always got your back,
just believe in me,
that's all I ask.

Bella

My dear,
your mum in small,
my love in whole,
knowing the world before the challenges you will
face.

I've always prayed you be free with me,
tell me your worries,
let me tell you the ways of boys,
men,
not holding back,
giving the truth so you prepared,
are confident to ask me,
have 100 percent trust in me,
this all I can give,
my love,
my experience,
your dad who has done lots and seen more,
always by your side no matter what been said,
my love for you never dead;
you are my daughter,
believe in me.

Brenden

My last born,
(as I am),
you are me,
independent like me
don't know what you do but be yourself,
live your truth,
independent mind flown,
you are me,
I miss you too much,
my mini me.

Free-Minded

My greatest responsibility as a parent is to enable, foster and nurture my child to be free-minded.

With a free heart of acceptance nothing is impossible.
This is why people fight,
go to war,
make the ultimate sacrifice,
to give others freedoms to be who they are,
who they want to be.

With freedom of the mind there is no mountain too high to climb or sea too rough to swim.
With a confidence that's steel clad,
there's no barb,
no challenge that can't be overcome,
but an inner fire that will never,
can never be extinguished.

With an open mind,
you won't waste energy on the unnecessary as freedom is the tonic.

Freedom enables a meraki life,
a willingness to live life to the fullest,
through understanding,
attaining,
living your ikigai.

My challenge as a parent is to take,
make hard decisions with sisu levels of confidence,
to lead a free life myself,
to be free-minded and lead by example.

House into a Home

You have a dream…

You buy a caravan to live and a plot to build a
house in a meadow,
up a mountain,
by the lake,
in the city,
near the beach.

Complete the legal paperwork,
architect a design,
buy materials,
hire labour,
start constructing.

Dig a hole,
put in foundations,
flatten floors and erect walls,
add a roof;
you now have a house.

Install wires and plumbing,
lights and skirting,
tiles and kitchen cabinets,
fitted wardrobes,
bath tubs,
washbasins and toilets.

Move in.
Buy tables and chairs,
beds,
a TV and fridge,
hang photos and paintings;
the house is turning into a home.

The final ingredients:
noisy children,
crying babies,
barking dogs,
a lioness by your side;
my dream now reality.

Morning Rush

Beep, Beep, Beep!
I bleary-eyed search for the alarm clock –
6:25am;
I hit the snooze button.

Beep, Beep, Beep!
five minutes later…
this time I have no choice.
Seven hours after jumping under covers,
snuggling up to my babe for a night of spooning,
I emerge from hibernation.

Open the bedroom door,
plod to the bathroom,
the start of another day.

Wake up you lazy bunch,
I shout as I knock on the kids' door.
On second calling, they appear,

tired like their old man.
Brush your teeth,
I remind.

Dad,
I can't find my socks, shoes or schoolbooks
comes the chorus as I relax under scalding shower to refresh my soul for the day ahead.

Miraculously,
by 7:05am,
only one child crying,
the kids all in the kitchen cereal box opening,
milk spilling.

One has no shoes,
another no socks,
the third doing yesterday's homework.

For fifteen minutes there's a hive of activity,
of squabbling,
complaining,
hair-raising.

A teacup gets broken,
the dog steals a slice of toast,
his tail wagging as he licks marmalade from tiles,
,

Socks and hoes found,
homework finished,
we leave the house only three minutes late,
the children munching as they jump in the car.

The three minutes has a knock-on effect –
the traffic that little bit heavier.
Annoyed I've missed the news,
I'm cheered by one of my favourite songs.

I drop the twins at pre-school,
kiss them on the forehead
and get back in the motor.

Next, the eldest.
He recites a nonsense story for the six-minute drive;
I listen happy in his happiness before he rushes excitedly,
waving and shouting to friends;
I'm happy to see his happiness.

Now peace as I crawl in the rush-hour traffic,
content my small ones are making their way joyfully through life.

I park the car,
put on my jacket,
grab my work bag,
walk through the front doors of the café,
my office.

Up a flight of steps to my usual table;
I'm ready to face the day ahead.

I don't know what stresses lie in wait,
but, I'm strong in my conviction and will do
whatever I need for the future of my family.

Responsibility

My kids equal love;
nothing else to say,
no explanation needed.

The oldest, the strongest,
a mountain of a man to come.
His quiet ways,
enjoying reading,
loving food.
He climbs trees like a baboon and swims like a fish;
he is the king of cartoons.

My crazy cat.
Her cheeky smile,
always joking at dad's expense:
You dance like Mr Bean!
Your music is slow like a turtle!

People say, she's a mini-mum.
My twin daughter,
a photogenic poser,
girlish but strong like her brothers.
She doesn't run from fights but goes head first
into the maelstrom of sibling rivalry.

The last born,
taking his time on all things babyish:
teething, walking, speaking.
He enjoys the attention of elders,
and when they don't pay him attention he'll bash,
scratch and smash them on the head.

I can't talk about my little ones without mentioning my wife;
only she can show a mother's love and make my
children who they are.

Bank Holiday Weekend

A bank holiday weekend-
no wife,
three children,
God, help me!

I talk to friends,
research the internet,
eventually strike gold –
I hope.

Early lasagne lunche,
stop at the ATM,
check the map,
two hours later we arrive.

First impressions,
mixed.

Park the car,
boot unpacked,
swimsuits on,
smiles and laughter in the air,
kids having the time of their lives.

Swimming, the sun, bouncy castle,
table tennis and walking;
by 6pm we're all exhausted.

We eat,
watch a cartoon film,
sleep.

Next day, the same.
Adventure nearly over,
our last morning,
one last splash in the pool,
then in the car and drive home.

It's been 48 life-affirming hours,
I'm now ready to face my uncertain future.

Day at the Beach

The alarm clock goes,
breakfast and then beach.

The engine started,
into gear,
reverse out garage,
through gate,
onto highway.

Mum and dad put on old, boring music,
we fight on the back seat,
play eye-spy,
I went to the market and bought...
then sleep.

We're at the beach,
swim,
beat up sharks,
build humongous castles,
dig tunnels and eat ice-cream.

Exhausted,
we fall into magical dreams.

House Party

Afternoon,
life relaxed,
men watching the match,
women cackling,
children playing hide-and-seek,
all getting mentally,
physically,
emotionally prepared for the evening,
the birthday braai.

R'n'B on car stereo,
four generations sitting outside talking,
two drinking one dancing.

A family get-together,
impromptu,
the best sort,
spontaneous,
this is living,
children enjoying
all chatting.

Time moves forwards,
the sun drops,
drinks consumed,
snacks shared,
the bouncy castle up,
sound system relocated outside.

Friends and family reunited,
waiting for guests,
partying,
drinking,
sexy-boy dancing,
girl twerking,
much laughing,
hopefully no vomiting.

The sun sinking,
light fading,
braai smoking,
hours quickly passing.

Chicken and beef in the air,
beer flowing like wine as we joke about the past,
don't worry about the morrow,
only living for the now.

The beats start,
this the signal to get jiggy with Big Willy,
Strength of a Women,
Murder she Wrote,
Gangsters Paradise
Mr Loverman...
shaba.

Classics,
the choir singing,
favourite dance moves reappearing,
granny dancing.

Stars high,
spirits up,
bottles emptying,
dance floor filling,
tunes mesmerising,
ass shaking,
lights not blinding,
joints passing,
shoving and shouting,
but no fighting,
this is house partying.

Soon the finish,
memories made,
family gathering ended,
smiles on faces,
moon start to fade.

Guests leave as beds are welcomed,
electrics back in boxes,
empties in crates,
chill out tunes quietening,
waiting for the sunrise and the party resuming.

Fucked up families

My family,
your family;
all fucked up.

Uncle Jack,
head of crack.

Auntie Helena,
full of bulimia.

Granny Clover,
an Irish rover.

Granddad Matt,
straight as a bat.

Nephew Roger,
topped up with vodka.

Uncle Stan,
a ladies man.

Cousin Jim,
full of sin.

Aunty Susan,
a dirty virgin.

Cousin John,
full of scorn.

Gay cousin Scott,
likes it up his bot.

My family,
your family;
all fucked up.

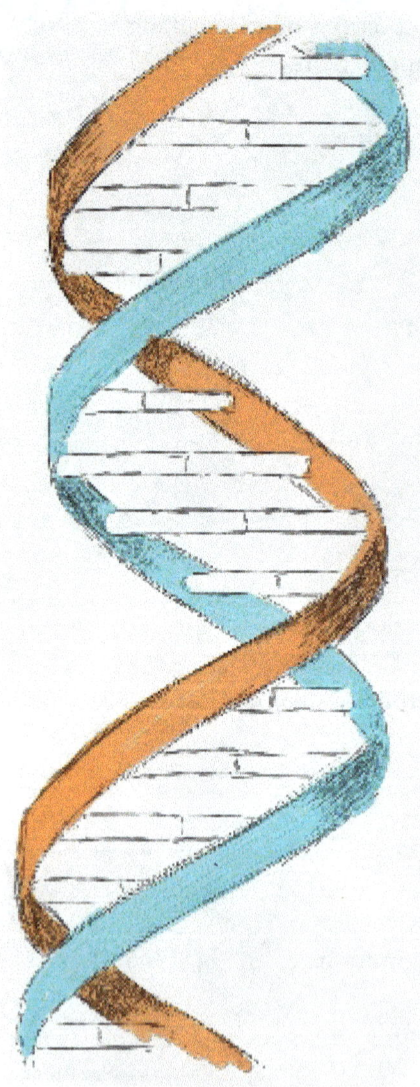

Doing a Flier

We met,
we loved,
we had such hopes.

We married,
had kids,
so much to lose.

I tried to live my ideals,
take the stress of love,
be the family provider,
the hard decisions all mine.

I was as you saw me,
didn't have much other than a willing heart,
you had expectarions
more than your reservations.

I let you stand on my shoulders to lift you up,
but you have pushed me down,
down into the ground.

You are controlling,
accusing,
not loving,
friending,
this lead to splintering,
seperaring,
finally divorcing,
no longer, I your life reserve.

I couldnt offer what you wanted-
security or adventure,
it's not possible to have both.

I couldn't match your goals,
not the father that you thought your dad was…
no matter all the bad he did to you!

You made me feel worthless,
useless,
adding nothing to your life,
you became a shadow wife!

Found acceptance in others,
they understanding my situation,
my misery,
not asking much other than smiles,
this led to short-term loving,
friendings with benefiting,
not committing,
I knew my boundaries.

You've bought me down,
now time for change,
to go back into town,
find a real life pirate,
one that's accepting,
has realistic expectations,
not love fluctuations.

If you want court wars,
bring it on!
Emotions obliterated,
future friendship gone,
I will not always stay calm,
peaceful,
quiet anymore,
time to be noisy,
unrelenting,
unforgiving,
you breaking my heart,
trying to financially ruin me,
but you'll not step on my soul anymore,
and I can bring your down,
you, a clown full of lies,
brain like a mince pie.

I can open doors into your mind,
expose your true character,
manipulator,
liar,
now I'm the one doing the flier,
leaving toxic in rear view mirror…
see what you've thrown away!

Shit Show

I'm in a bar,
having a jar,
maybe two,
three,
ten,
i don't know,
my heart is torn,
I'm forlorn,
life unbeliveable,
how can you be so destructible,
one whirlwind creating such chaos,
an utter shit show,
emotional firestorm,
just for disbelieving,
disceiving,
you want family disrobing,
just for own rationalising,
this is mentaling,
kids destroying,
don't know,
but seems you been bad receving of advice,
think I'm all vice,
reality,
I loved you heart triced,
you thrown all away,
think I'm gay,
bi-sexual,
you, of your crazual,
need remedial,
what the fuck you up to,
trying to win,
pointing fingers that all I do is sin,
the truth,
you turn and poison,
children refuse,
make me recluse,
police accuse of abuse,
think i'm obtuse,
but end of day....
you'll lose,
realise what lost can't be found again,
no regain,
I'll refrain,
children, for your sake,
I hope will restrain,
forgive and still love you for the shit show you've
singuarly created.

WE GROW OLDER

In life, two certainties prevail: taxes and death. The inevitability of the hereafter looms whether it's sooner or later. At times, this knowledge can seem overwhelming and makes living seem so damn difficult, confusing and contradictory. We find ourselves questioning why we compromise our individual needs in pursuit of harmony. Is this even humane?? Is this questioning the essence of being human?

Such contemplation makes me reappraise the concept of the final curtain. I acknowledge death. Whether tomorrow or in a thousand years, and regardless of technological advancements or medical breakthroughs, there will eventually be an end, a finality. That being the case, it's better I accept (death) rather than pretend it will never happen. Time, too, moves inexorably forward, sparing no one from the grasp of aging and the responsibilities that come with it. No one is a forever young gun. All become older with responsibilities to others and oneself.

One can attempt to push back the passage of time like King Canute holding back the tide, but history has shown us the futility of such endeavours, how that story ends. The reality, to someone under twenty-five, even though I'm mid-forties, I'm a relatively old fart whose belly is extending. I'm no longer the lithe whipper-snapper of yesteryears, more a portly Labrador with a grey flecked nozzle showing my true age no matter how shinny and silky my coat. As such, I think it is far healthier, no pun intended, to talk about dying rather than it being taboo. By embracing the inevitable we can prepare ourselves and face the process of growing old with dignity. Admitting the inevitable means I don't need to be alone when it happens. This realisation is important. It means I can find peace with myself and those I leave behind. I can build deep and lasting connections which transcend epitaphs or photographs. I can also plan my affairs rather than leaving a shitstorm in my wake for others to clean up. These are existential questions to the human condition. By acknowledging and embracing these realities, we can navigate our journey with a sense of purpose, understanding, and the opportunity to leave a positive imprint on the lives of others. In facing death with dignity and openness, we can find solace, connection, and meaning amidst the transient nature of our existence.

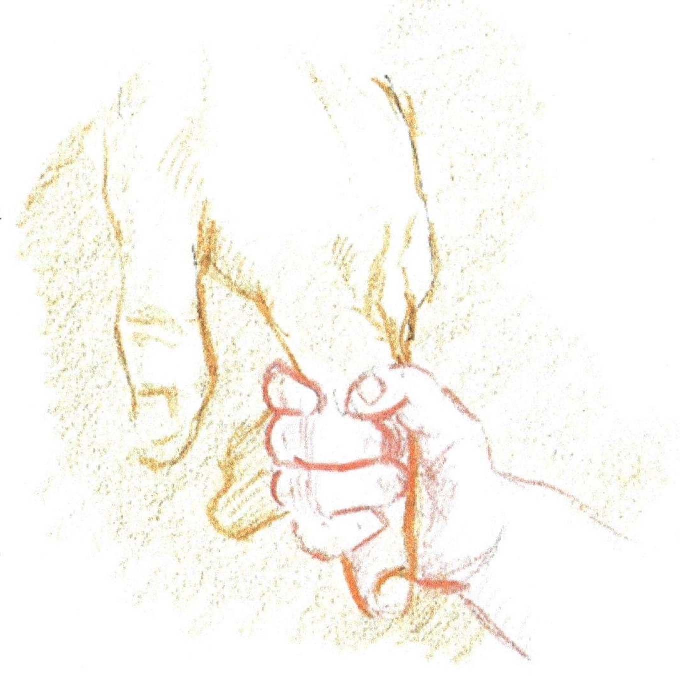

Dying Day

If this is to be my dying day...
I want to die easy,
the devil by myside.
I will not rage against the dying of the light,
nor have regrets for living my way.

If this is to be my dying day...
I will drink like a fish,
pub crawl to the cemetery,
take shooters and find enlightenment in absinthe
with strangers who become drinking buddies;
I will have no regrets living my way.

If this is to be my dying day...
I will get high as a kite and see space dragons,
get loved up and be mellow yellow;
I will have no regrets living my way.

If this is to be my dying day...
I will live life like a sailor,
a soldier on R&R,
a top gun fly boy;
death and danger,
many a comrade,
no stranger;
I will have no regrets living my way.

If this is to be my dying day...
I will casino like James Bond,
flutter on the nags,
bet on football and play poker with friends;
I will have no regrets living my way
If this is to be my dying day...
I will fuck a girl in every city,
every position,
every hole.
I will live with a red light my companion,
romance the nurse,
have one night stands and break hearts;
I will have no regrets living my way.

If this is to be my dying day...
I will pass on lessons learned.
I will articulate,
contemplate and educate my children so they don't fall into the same traps as I;
I will have no regrets living my way.

If this is to be my dying day...
I will practice that life has no full stops,
so take one step at a time.
That there is no time to waste,
and love is all that counts;
I will have no regrets living my way.

I will not judge so don't judge me,
positivity is the way to be.
I will tackle each situation on its merits,
and accept that life is about decisions and mistakes.
I will own mine,
I alone accountable for my actions,
my choices;
I will have no regrets living my way.

If this is to be my dying day...
I know the best laid plans of mice and men oft go a glade.
I will rise above the chaos and treat life as a marathon not a sprint.

Know, that we each have a life to lead,
immeasurable equations to handle,
and that life has many ambiguities;
I will have no regrets living my way.

If this is to be my dying day...
I want to die easy,
friends by my side.
I will not rage against the dying of the light,
nor have regrets living my way.

My Generation...

No longer am I a youth with parents,
a young man with friends,
but an aged geezer contemplating the passing of time.

Down the ages I've played kiss chase,
spin the bottle and numerous drinking games,
but now,
bridge,
relaxation not razzmatazz,
mind games not mind-fucked.

Now I live for smiles on my children's faces,
on shorty's,
no more chasing vices.

I smile for the upturn in my fortunes,
for small comforts,
finding meaning in my life,
making it through the day,
watching the moon glisten and sun rise.
showing kindness in smiles.

Mid-Life

Is this what getting older means?
Where once life was care free,
everything now has consequence.

Where before all I worried about was me,
now I worry about others.

Where before I could...
drink what I wanted,
sleep with who I could and work when I pleased...
now when I drink,
I get a hangover and lose my job
If I sleep around,
I get divorced.

I'm older and have more responsibilities,
this is the cycle of life;
no work no money for lazy man.

Care free days gone forever,
the elixir of youth passing its sell-by date as I cry for my yesteryear.

Getting Older

Getting older,
who would wish it on anyone?
The pain in our joints,
kidneys and soul comes and goes like a ghost,
a fart in the wind;
I'm afraid to investigate,
get a prognosis.

My big hair,
big cheeks,
big legs,
good eyes,
mince pies,
this, what has physically defined me,
what I used to see in the mirror.

Now,
as I write this poem,
my eyes can't focus.
I've had a few beers as I scribe,
but even stone cold sober,
I can no longer see text,
it's all a blur.

My eyesight was 20/20
no need for glasses or contact lenses,
something I took for granted…
how I literally saw the world,
now deserting me.

My hearing,
never 100% now getting worse;
smelling and touching
hard to tell except when kinky blindfolding.

My body is changing after a lifetime of living.
Cells getting older,
decades of drinking all catching up.

My physical future uncertain,
poorer eyes impacting my daily reality,
my subconscious as I enter the second half of
my life.

When I wake from dreams,
that millisecond of consciousness,
I don't know whether my day,
my back,
will be pain free or I'll be bent-double,
walking like the geriatric I'm soon to become.

How many pain killers?
the usual question to start my day.
I evolve strategies:
no heavy boxes,
don't go to the gym,
but this is not me –
I want to lift weights and cradle children without
crying in discomfort.

Getting older is a misery!
Can I accept this literal fading of the light as I
move ever closer to my final curtain,
all my senses failing,
my body only good for donating,
cremating,
life's sensations coming to cessation,
ruination,
finalization!

Vertigo

I'm walking,
I'm fine,
all is normal,
something is happening,
room spinning,
I've not been smoking,
drinking,
all day good feeling.

Balance gone,
not drunk a beer much less bottle tequila...
but holding walls,
going to fall over,
seeing triple;
what the fuck's going on?

My legs gone pins and needles,
I'm wearing jelly shoes,
can't see straight let alone walk a line.

Stumble to table,
slump sweating into chair,
confused,
the world utterly chaotic,
don't know what's going on,
I'm getting scared.

What's happening?
Is this a heart attack,
stroke,
some other mystery illness?
Its appeared from nowhere,
left me utterly debilitated.

Focus on a single spot,
need to concentrate,
the world slowing,
my breathing less hyperventilating,
start shivering,
sweat turning me freezing.

Life more normal,
surroundings not moving,
I must get going,
find a safe place to lie down,
rest,
recuperate,
let my body and brain reach equilibrium,
recharge before another vertigo turn.

The Assassin

Roadblocks set up,
traffic halted and motorists inconvenienced for presidential ego,
flashing police lights approaching along deserted highway.

I view this through hotel window as I drink an ice-cold water,
eat peanuts and watch football on the TV.
I'm being inconspicuous,
Mr. Everyday,
a nobody of consequence.

I'm as serene as a cobra while I calmly survey my surroundings.
I feel the cold of the gun pressing into the small of my back,
ready to spit its 9mm venom.

Brain is switched on,
senses alert,
muscle fibres twitching,
waiting to explode into life at the sound of my starting pistol.

How did I change from teacher and family man…
to assassin?
What has my country driven me to?

The presidential convoy arrives:
thirty vehicles, fifty soldiers, a helicopter, an ambulance, bodyguards, minions and coat-tail grabbers.

Through the foyer they approach en-masse,
the entourage invading,
I mentally rehearsing my moves.

The President only twenty metres,
five seconds before life will change forever,
until it will fatally end.

I grab the butt of the gun and feel the reassuring weight.

Five meters.

Life flashes in front of my eyes;
there's no turning back,
I'm at peace whatever comes next.

I shoot.
I shoot again,
and again,
and again;
three bullets hitting their mark as I wish they had
when soldiers raped my wife,
my children forced to watch.

Everything moves in slow motion.
Bodyguards raise their weapons as I run to the exit on my left,
peanuts uneaten on the counter.

I feel a stabbing pain in my shoulder,
and then another;
I've been hit!

I stumble,
adrenalin keeps pumping legs.
My chest explodes,
leg folds;
I can't run anymore.

I wheeze,
bloody bubbles froth from mouth;
my time now near.

Soon, I'll be reunited with my family,
living a happy and peaceful life on a small farm in the sky,
the heat of the day on my skin,
my children playing with smiles on their faces,
my wife watching proudly on.

I close my eyes and walk peacefully towards my future,
my past,
my family,
towards the light at the end of the tunnel.

I'm going home,
reunited with the love taken from me…
but which I've stopped being stolen from others.

CIRCLE OF LIFE

Have you ever been woken by the sun shining through the curtains? At times, this is highly annoying as it disturbs slumber. Yet, there are moments when you don't want anything interrupting the tranquillity of this perfect moment. Occasionally, your head might be doing cartwheels as you think with vivid recollections of the previous day, every second etched in crystal clarity. You said, goodbye to someone for a final time as they passed into the afterlife (if there is one). You don't know if there is anyone or anything that will or could help you get through the next minutes, days, weeks or months. Will there be someone who can save you from yourself as you enter grief, a period of mourning? It is the point when you can't take anything from death apart from hurt and anguish. Where time is not yet a healer, the emotion still too raw, solace feels elusive and the pain cuts deep. But, the sunbeam can carry a deeper metaphor for life continuing. It symbolises life going from one day to the next, nothing and no one able to stop the continuum, halt the forward march of time. Whether Christian, Muslim, Jew Atheist or other philosophical belief, all inherently recognise this fundamental truth. Life might seem like it stops with the death of someone, but it doesn't; death is the red light but life is forever green. As the sunbeam shines through, you are faced with a choice of how to live. Do you give yourself a chance to love again, life persistently moving forward? I repeat- there is life after death; your life! The sunrays of hope, love and possibility are always present and can guide you through the journey of existence.

The 7 Ages of Time

What is time,
when time you don't know?

Time,
when time seems so slow?

Then the present,
the purest glow.

The birth of another,
a future light show.

The past,
becomes an afterglow.

The dimming off the light,
so slow.

What is time,
when death doth bestow?

Last Goodbye

5 weeks,
4 countries,
met friends old and new,
increased my business network;
a time of productive days and fun nights,
some never to be forgotten.

Kenya,
the East African economic heartbeat.
Meetings galore,
much achieved,
Nairobi left peeved,
Kisumu magic weaved.

Uganda,
no rough diamond.
Chaos, bad roads and constant horns...
but,
it felt natural in the hotel cum brothel.
Not somewhere I would choose to live,
but was greeted with friendship,
had first time experiences.

Rwanda,
just a few, but unforgettable days.
New feelings created,
hope to be repeated,
currently relegated.

24 hours in Egypt.
The Sphinx,
pyramids and mummies,
a river cruise on the Nile,
sleeping in airports as I rush home.

Life will change soon,
big decisions to make on work,
family,
death,
legal issues.

I say goodbye to Africa for now,
hope reunited soon.
I'm on my way to see dad,
maybe one last time.

I leave,
not with trepidation of the unknown,
but excitement of adventures to come.
Will these be my last words to my father,
he who has given me the strength,
courage to live life to my own rules,
on my own terms?
I might not always be successful,
but life is never dull.

No matter the sadness of the circle of life,
it is only contemplating death we realise how
important it is to embrace life,
to live to the fullest;
one day it will end,
this as sure as taxes.

The finish line may take time or be sudden,
so, have no regrets of things not done,
decisions not made.
Live your true self,
temet nosce,
one day it will be over and I'll be saying a last
goodbye,
my ashes blowing in the wind.

Memories

A grey hair here,
there,
everywhere;
I'm still life aware,
but time passing me by.

My teens and early twenties,
halcyon days,
no responsibilities,
always on a high.
While others were studious…
chasing pussy was my bachelors,
acting the drunken fool… my PhD.

The Friday night bar crawl,
mistrust and aggression,
piled-up nightclubbing to sunrise,
chatting up MILFs and fingering jailbait,
starting unprovoked fights in equal displays of
bravado and stupidity.

We were, boys on holidays,
our anthem,
"lager, lager, lager"
We didn't care about tomorrow,
only living for today.

I still listen to music,
I can move my feet,
but this is a young person's game,
I a grey-haired drunken warrior.

When I was a child,
I spoke as a child,
I understood as a child,
I thought as a child:
but when I became a man,
I put away childish things
did my own thing,
no more bling.

As an increasingly belly spreading man,
I'm jealous of the beauty of youth,
the veracity of life,
the elixir of my former self.

The Present is the Past and Future

Back to the Future,
spaceships and androids,
Star Trek and Red Dwarf,
A Space Odyssey –
these my childish adolescence,
of concept theorizing,
popcorn eating,
futuristic impossibilities.

But that future is now,
here.

Is there difference between The Matrix and virtual reality?
Hunger Games and African refugees entering Europe?
Self-driving cars and the Google encyclopaedia;
Elon Musk is Ironman!

My dreams and childish drawings now augments reality,
interspatial banality,
unintelligible finality,
galactic neutrality.

The future is now,
the present is back to my future,
the past an analogue world long forgotten,
a time my binary children can't comprehend,
a black and white life foreign to them.

This present,
my past,
has realised my childish future imagination.

Granddad

You are my grandfather,
grandad,
papa,
opa.

My mum's father.
you, her hero,
she, your little girl,
she, worshiping at your feet.

I know you as a good man,
pillar of the community,
businessman who put family first,
this is what I've been told...
but once you were my age,
a teenager,
freedom in the world for the first time-
a Nazi youth.

I know this is nurture,
but how much nature?
What stories and horrors have you not told,
that you can't reveal from embarrassment,
self-fulfilment,
sorrow,
pride,
maybe, jail banishment?

Who is the real you?
What is deep in your soul?
Are you atoning or hiding in plain sight?
Are these questions to simple for the human psyche,
your experiences unbelievable,
untenable,
un-understandable to someone who has been brought up as me?

I don't want to nominate,
castigate,
flagellate,
point fingers and regurgitate,
as I haven't lived your life,
but I want to know who you really are,
this, to help me understand who I am,
where I've come from,
I, both nature and nurture.

You are,
were an influence on my mum,
you and my mother moulding me.

You are part of me,
good and bad,
happy and sad;
this, the meaning of family.

Friends you find but relations are largely what makes you;
like it or not,
rebel or accept,
there is no running from the past for both of us.

Mum, Mother, Ma

My mum, my wife, my daughter,
three generations of women caring for me,
their son, husband, father.

I have female affections,
I'm lucky to have three women in my life,
each with their idiosyncrasies,
the same but so different.

To my mother,
I'm the little munchkin,
the bundle of pink,
the boy who can do no wrong no matter all the bad I do.

My wife,
I stole your innocence.
I am your husband, lover and father to our children.

To my daughter,
I am god,
the fountain of knowledge, laughter and money;
I mould the world to my will.

Mums know on their son's wedding day,
another will become more important…
but if my wife grows into my ma,
as a husband, I've picked well.

And one day,
you, my daughter,
will have a new man to worship…
if you becomes like your mum,
my wife should be congratulated.

I'm neither cherub, caveman nor god,
just me,
being who I am,
doing what I do,
with who I want,
but influenced by these ladies three.

As a boy, man, husband and father,
I give thanks for the women in my life,
for the love you all give and the lessons you've taught me.

Aging

Time comes and goes.
it passes,
we but actors,
the world a stage.

We have parents,
grandparents,
one day that will be us,
the body and mind fragile,
this, an inescapable fact,
part of the life story.

There is no running away from truth no matter riches.
Once beautiful bodies,
smiles,
will sag,
amazing minds will go childish.

I see this truth in the eyes of the old,
their life force fading
joys now simple:
TV and food,
seeing children,
grandchildren,
the circle of life in its simplicity.

The days no longer of exploration and exhilaration,
laughter and tears,
now monotony,
being poked and prodded by doctors,
body failing,
waiting one day not to wake up.

We all return to whence we came,
dust on the wind,
buried under the earth,
figments of remembrance,
only the memory of who we were living on.

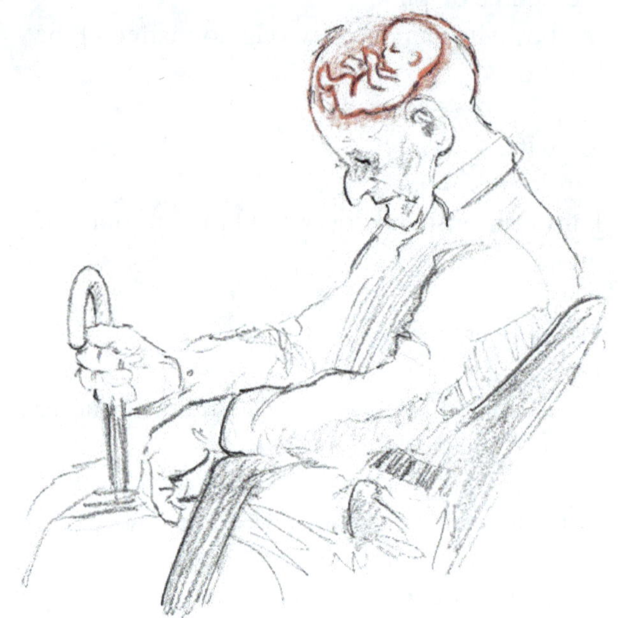

Legacy

Hold me like a warm embrace,
a song of love,
for the hurt I feel of what I leave behind.

A life worth living is a life lived.

I've seen much and done more
think I've done ok.
children brought up,
making their way,
keeping life going with smile on faces.

Choices I made,
regrets a few,
chances not taken,
hardships worn and broken hearts healed.

We get one life,
one chance to do what you think is correct,
though there is no right or wrong,
just decisions,
a life of choices
the 51% what I'm accountability for,
this more good than bad,
positive than negative,
opportunity rather than debilitating challenge.

As my time nears,
I consider,
reflect:
who have my children grown into being?
What sort of parent will they be?
Will their children respect them?
This, my legacy.

Knockin' on Heaven's Door

I'm born a babe into this unintelligible world,
a life of daily new experiences,
my senses tested and constantly refined,
my immune system building…
but when I got chicken pox,
the fragility of life laid bared…
I thought I would be knockin' on heaven's door.

As a teenager I lived life big,
to imbibe anything and everything:
alcohol,
girls,
class A's,
magical love,
depression.
I was finding my way in life and lucky to survive
the train crash…
I was not ready to knock on heaven's door.

In mid-life I decided which bridges to cross and
burn;
I inevitably chose wrong.
The wrong marriage led to divorce.
The wrong investment led to financial ruin.
The wrong job led to unemployment.
The wrong bottle of pills…
kept me from knockin' on heaven's door.

Others,
friends and family,
too many to mention,
taken early.
Suicide,
cancer,
accident,
their suffering too much to bear…
before they knocked on heaven's door.

I have been given a second, a third chance.
Mistakes forgiven,
new relationships a joy.
My lover accepts my faults and foibles,
I, exalt in her for simply being she.

I have lived a full life,
seen much and done more.
I've loved and lost,
been thrilled and almost killed.
I stared death in the eyes but refused to be taken,
always living my days as if they were my last as
they are now…
I'm at peace and welcome knockin' on heaven's
door.

Death Stare

I stare,
I stare,
I remember.

Champagne days of early adulthood,
freedom and responsibilities,
a world I was entering but knew little about,
hopeful expectations,
no need justifications,
this what 20s all about.

I stare,
I stare,
I remember.

Enter my 30s,
family man,
did my best,
kids grew now children of their own;
one baby dead,
can never get her face outta my head.

I stare,
I stare,
I remember.

To my 40s,
life so full,
work and play,
never a dull day.

Live life to the fullest,
keep pushing hardest,
always feeling restless.

I stare,
I stare,
I remember.

I retire,
rewind,
relive my life,
always remind;
look back, not forward,
soon cremated on a rack.

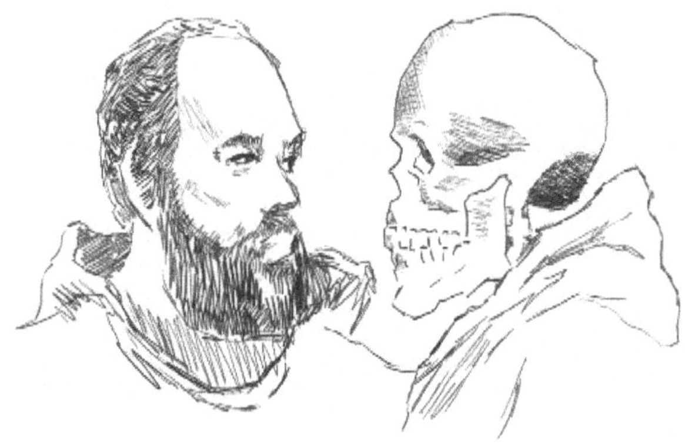

I stare,
I stare,
I remember.

Once I was king of hospitality,
life and soul of the party,
flirty,
tarty,
now Death stares back,
this, life circle parity.

The Final Journey

88 and this is my last breath,
the future I don't know,
thought about it a lot,
have faith,
but your guess as good as mine.

I have a last look at all I have known,
this world,
despite challenges generally been good to me.
Loving families through the ages,
interesting carrer and happy retirement,
I have no grumbles,
Few life stumbles,
the last year's less enjoyable,
my only fun in day-dreams and remembering a life lived.

But now I go,
dying in my house of 30 years,
pain no more,
all I know gone.

I'm covered by sheet,
hands over chest,
bubbles escaping my lips,
my life force,
soul, leaving the building,
I, Elvis no more.

Down stairs on a gurney,
carried out feet first as I wished,
my wife and sons looking on,
i pray they will be fine,
find solace in my passing,
move forward with their lives,
my passing not stopping the spinning of the world.

I go to the mortuary,
not been many before,
this what I'm least looking forward to.
I imagine its like going to the dentist or garage,
I put my faith in the skills of the mortician,
for them to give me back respect,
to somehow give those who see me in casket,
a final view of who I was years and not days back.

I'm on the final journey,
dressed smartly,
suit and regimental tie,
old school pin on as I cross The River Styx,
the barrier separating the living from the dead,
Hades,
the Underworld,
Erebus guarding the gateway.

The undertakers have done a good job,
money well spent,
now I'm ready for a final parade,
friends and family to attend my passing out.

Drawn on artillery carriage,
flag-bearers giving a final salute,
the funeral quicker than I imagined,
the army chaplain and catholic priest sending me on my way,
my boys words those that I will remember more.

As I travel to the creamtorium,
I wish I was at the golf club enjoying a pint of bitter and sandwiches with my friends and family,
but those times and no more for me;
I hope soon to see loved ones partying in the sky.

My final resting place,
ashes to ashes outside the Officers Mess,
the scene of so many fun times,
this where I will live on in memories,
I forever reciting poems,
sometimes revelry,
more often stupidity,
this life one of complexity,
but for me, thankability.

BACK TO THE EARTH

Death has a unique way of bringing the true essence of life into focus. It reminds us of our mortality and the importance of making the most of our time. The party finishes with a scattering of ashes, a pint of beer and a handful of vol-au-vents for the mourners. Accepting death allows for planning. I think, when I know my time is coming I will record myself so my kids, future generations can hear and see me. I would tell my kids how proud I am of them. I will remind them how much I love them and how, though I tried my best, I wish I could have been a better father. I would tell stories of happier times as I weave a tapestry of cherished memories. With honesty and vulnerability, I will share the lessons I've learned along my journey, hoping to guide them in their own lives.

I'll probably be having beer when speaking into the camera, this to help evoke a familiar scent that may trigger fond memories. I might show myself shaving, a simple act that once brought laughter and warmth as their tiny fingers tickled my neck, their soft cheeks brushing against my bristles. I would tell of the good times we had as a family, and some of the nonsense I got up to with my mates over the years. I would outline my success and failures, past romances and jobs that I'd done. I would talk about my brother, their uncle and other relations.

I would offer a set of guiding principles to navigate the complexities of life. I will advise them to learn from my mistakes. And of course, my poems are a digital legacy of my life in the raw. Maybe, subconsciously, this is the real motivation for my writing – a record of my days as I move towards my final resting place.

I'll openly discuss my views on death. That I don't believe in a God or the afterlife. That I don't want to be worm food but prefer to be turned into ashes. That I was not scared of the big decisions I've made down the years or being accountable for my screw ups I would admit to the fear and trepidation I felt in the waiting-room during their births, and how that fear has followed me throughout their lives. The weight of parental concern is a testament to our love and humanity, that being scared is the most human of parenting emotions. I would talk about love, religion, dogs, sex, alcohol, addictions, children, horses, football, rugby, cricket; you name it, anything that captures the breadth of existence. Ultimately, my message would centre around embracing the uncertainties of life, acknowledging that some things are beyond our control. I would encourage them to confront their fears, to live fully and authentically, and to embrace the precious gift of life.

Ashes to Ashes

I'll soon be resting…
but not six-feet down;
through my ashes,
I will live on in budding flowers.

My ashes will be spread in the earth,
on the ground you walk,
the fields you plough,
the soil used for life,

Earth,
the building block of life,
the nutrients for carbohydrates that feed live-
stock;
I'll cultivate the earth,
the land decomposing me!

The urn will be taken to my favourite spot,
here,
my life through decades.
No longer am I a boy with family or young man
with friends,
but an aged geezer by myself,
contemplating the passing of time.

I've been here through my ages:
kiss chase,
smoke behind the caravan,
dirty weekend,
now death is awaiting.

This piece of real estate that will be forever me,
that has witnessed my triumphs and disasters,
indiscretions and joy,
a place that can tell a thousand stories,
so many memories.

My ashes to be spread besides a favourite tree. Visitors to my final resting place will see the wonders of the world as they look out across the sea and can revel in the circle of life.

Back to the Earth

Will mine be glorious or quiet?
Over the top or under a blanket?
Through a maelstrom,
or just is…
a passing from here to there as I go back to the earth,
buried or cremated.

Death a finality,
the end life totality,
reconstituted compatibility,
as body decrying,
senses failing,
mind flapping,
wondering about humanity,
spiritually-
is there another reality?

Going back to the earth is no surprise
one we can't run from.
We don't know when,
where or how,
but the Grim Reaper will visit,
this as sure as taxes.

Death,
whether age,
cancer,
accident,
the random unexpected,
in an irony,
it being the only certainty;
everyone dies,
life, an unwinnable race.

But not everyone gets to live,
to love,
so I will rage,
rage against the dying of the light,
live the fullest till I die,
party to the end,
have no regrets on my rollercoaster of an adventure

I will live now,
love now,
be in the moment,
have no have regrets or over think mistakes,
fuckups and disappointments…
it's better to live wild and die young than old,
bitter and frustrated.
a life constipated when it's time to go back to the earth.

It's Been a Blast

And so,
this is it,
my final goodbye.

We know from a young age this day will come-a-knocking.
Whether death visits through old age or accident,
peaceful or violent,
there is no running from the circle of life.

I've seen many places,
experienced many cultures,
tasted many cuisines,
had a few loves and lovers,
many friends;
I hope I'll be remembered as a good person.

My heart will stop first,
my brain thereafter;
I'm ready, my time is shortly.

I accept no more sunrises,
these my last few seconds of life;
I don't know if there'll be nothing,
the pearly gates or a fiery hell to come.

I've brought up my children,
my DNA passed down the family line,
a little bit of me living on.
They seem happy,
doing well at school,
most importantly they are loved;
that's all I can ask for.

I've been to many funerals,
seen friends buried,
cremated and put on pyres,
each to their own belief.

Now is my time and soon I'll be blowing in the wind,
my ashes floating on my favourite lake,
loved ones seeing the wonders of this world.

I can see you at my coffin, weeping,
but don't gnash your teeth,
don't be morose.
I lived 100 miles per hour,
surrounded by noise and making even more;
now I want peace,
time to myself,
others the centre of attention.

Dressed in Black

I've been lucky,
not been to many funerals before.
Grandparents and elderly relatives,
their time on planet earth reaching its natural end,
an escape to aged suffering.

But my brother from another mother,
why?

The life and soul of every party,
not an enemy to be seen yet cut down in the prime of life.

Living life on the edge,
never saying, no,
always up for it,
whatever,
whoever,
whenever
IT, was.

He never took a backward step,
ran from a fight but rather always rescued friends.

How can his effervescence,
the very spirt of life be destroyed like a fragile flower,
the heat drained from his body?

We're at his favourite pub,
this, his second home for the wake.

He has a favourite drink in right hand,
pool cue in the left;
he would've enjoyed this send off,
his final party;
one day we will be reunited.

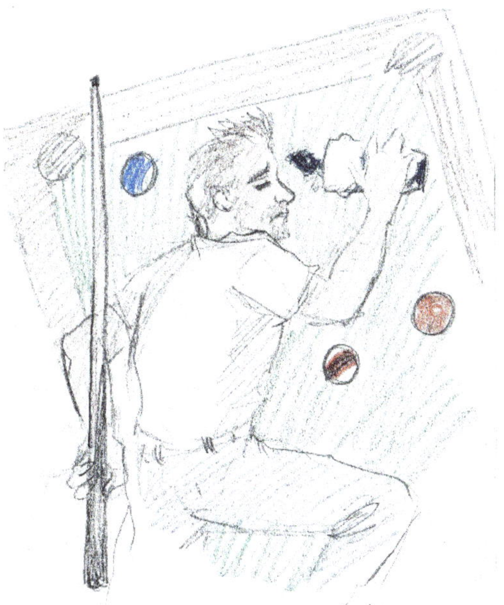

Tomorrow,
coffin on shoulders,
only the good die young;
I know he's not afraid to walk down the tunnel into his future.

God love him,
God bless him,
God keep my brother from another mother-
Rest In Peace.

My Child

You were my sunshine,
my life and my joy;
saying goodbye to you,
the hardest thing I'll ever do.

Rest In Peace.

Father

As you were at my birth,
I am at your death.
What you have done in-between,
defines who you are,
your legacy.

We didn't always agree.
Sometimes, I didn't understand your reasoning or you mine,
but now, I, as a dad realize you were both individual and father,
that you only wanted the best for me.

You taught me the most important of lessons-
what it means to be a father,
to have your child's back,
to be their pillar when things go wrong,
even when you disagree.

No matter our difference of opinion,
you were there for me in times of good or bad,
always guiding my course of action;
I contemplating, what would dad do?

We went to the same school that you enjoyed so.
You taught me a love of theatre,
poems and writing diaries.
You introduced me to golf, snooker, cricket,
bridge and travelling,
to be kind to animals,
that dogs are man's best friend.

What it means to serve,
we both cadets,
you a lifetime,
38 years of putting others before yourself,
I, 18 months as a Royal Signals reservist and getting some taste of friends going to war.

You were the centre of the party-
in the officer's mess,
golf club, bridge club,
family get-together,
not because you craved attention but all were
drawn to your good humour,
your generous soul,
your amusing views on life's idiosyncrasies;
you set the example that not just I,
but many want to emulate.

I see you now resting in your house of 30 years.
You are at peace,
cold to the touch but not in pain,
once more calm,
not fighting the dying of the light.

You are surrounded by what you love,
5 generations of photos looking down on you.
Images of army and books of cricket,
the queen,
beer mats and tea cups.
This is what made you,
my father
you who made me.

You are marched out from home one last time,
feet first as you wished,
to be drawn on your beloved 25-Pounder,
family and friends to honour,
remember you.
As you were at my birth
I am at your death.
Goodbye,
and thank you for being you,
for being dad.

The Sun will Rise

Life will stop.
You'll think there is no tomorrow.
You don't know how you will carry on.

You have lost what you loved,
you think it is irreplaceable,
you don't know what will fill the void.

You flounder,
you worry,
you cry yourself to sleep.

But tomorrow the sun will rise
and who knows what the tide will bring in?

You will survive,
you will be stronger and what you achieve will be in our memory;
you will live our dream.

The impact you have on others will be like the sun that never sets;
from adversity comes courage and love.

You are our strength.
Give hope to others-
you now have the power of two in one.

Your loss is your love,
your love is your kindness,
your kindness is what you have to offer,
your offer is what others want –
to feel your love continue.

The sun will set and when you see the moon
know I will be there,
to guide you through life and to the hereafter;
I'm in the stars and will always by your side.

Though we are apart,
we will live on in each other's love and the joy of all those who know us.

Always believe in our love.
Never give up;
together,
two in one.

Glad to Have Known You

We are sad for your leaving,
though happy we knew you;
for your time on earth,
our lives are richer.

We saw you at your brightest-
the star of the show,
the centre of the party,
the leader amongst peers,
the first amongst equals.

I am relieved you're no longer in pain;
my friend,
go rest.

As you reach for the stars find the moon;
go and meet others who've passed before with
smile on your face.

You,
always looking fly,
always a good word,
a good heart.
doing things your way,
in your style,
in your time,
but time gone too soon.

Your funeral,
the last we will see each other…
but your memory will live on
in the hearts of all you knew.

Your final resting place, says everything:
your appreciation of the world,
the wonders we live through each day;
even in death you still make smiles.

My brother from another mother,
the world is poorer for your passing;
you are missed but will never be forgotten.
Rest In Peace.

Sister

My sister,
same mister but I never knew,
your passing before I arriving,
a life I never saw but always felt,
a gap from my life experience,
not before,
but maybe I should have seen you as my guardian angel,
I, living for both of us.

Doubled,
is that why I'm so troubled,
never finding peace,
always inner conflict,
not mindful space,
a never-ending mental race?

I live my truth,
but heart never rest,
you,
my sister,
seeing the worst and best.

Last six months,
dad in a hearse,
children gone missing,
I'm a ship,
pure leaking,
almost sinking,
but will somehow keep going,
this my only known,
positiviting,
forward thinking,
doing my best for both of us.

I know I have many mistakes,
terrible pancakes,
but I'm true,
and your missing make me cry for the sister I didn't know,
a life taken from me,
this, the unfortunate reality,
cruelty.

Perhaps, we'd be friends,
soulmates,
adventurers,
or not...
that why family you born and friends you make,
cake bake.

But, when I look it all,
I hear dad's prayer,
make me cry like I don't know,
only you,
the one who lives above me,
can see the truth.

You're my guardian angel not hole in the heart,
you early depart but still live on,
I, now seeing it for that!

You're in new friends and words,
helping to open my eyes,
this world somehow explain,
see the beauty in new reality,
liveability,
I, two-in-one.

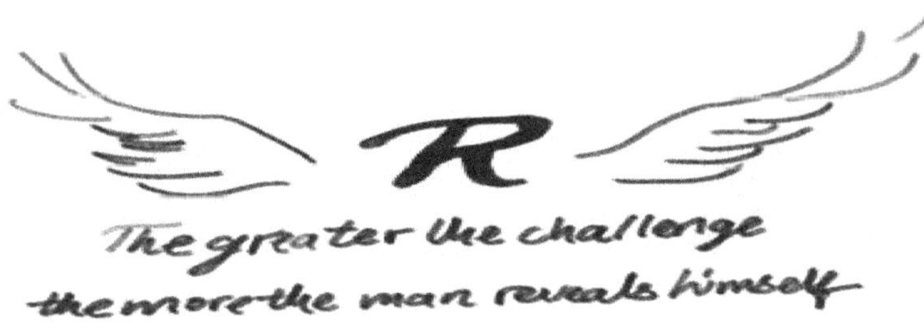

IS THIS THE MEANING OF LIFE?

Like you, I'm not sure what lies ahead. What will happen next week, the rest of this year, over the next decade or when it'll be time to meet our maker? We, all of us, are not able to change the past and so have no choice but to live in the now, the present. Life has taught me the cliché: live each second as if it's your last, for it's in the present that true living occurs.

What I've found out, is that during our life journey we will face impossible decisions, where there's a hair's breadth between going left or right, forward or backwards, crossroads where the slightest deviation can have profound consequences. In these moments, whatever you do will have both positive, negative and utterly unknown consequences. As Donald Rumsfeld eloquently put it, "… there are known knowns; there are things we know we know. We also know there are known unknowns; that is to say we know there are some things we do not know. But there are also unknown unknowns — the ones we don't know we don't know." This is life! To that end, we have to often make very difficult, life-changing decisions with incomplete, limited or conflicting information.

Navigating these complexities means we must recognize that the outcome of our choices is not solely determined by the inherent goodness or badness of them. We should not think of the end result and conclude, that the best decisions led to the best outcomes and worst to worst. This is simplistic, result-based rationale and which can be debilitating; you can make a good decision that gets a bad result and vice versa. I propose, embrace a mind-set to willingly live with being accountable for the consequences in the knowledge that things might not go according to plan. So, venture into uncharted territories, take calculated risks and embrace the unknown unknowns; live as a life pirate!

Life Pirate

I've been around the world thrice,
married twice,
but only found a home once.

I've seen a man with 2 penises,
a crazy cat saxophone man,
and a ladyboy with her man toy.

A man with charisma,
my best friend,
saved me from a beating;
my North Star
saved me from myself.

But what is the meaning of life?
What is the meaning to your life?

Is it the family you're born to,
kids that you procreate or friends meet?

Is it accumulating riches or celebrating challenges overcome?

And what about the highs you were afraid to ascend
and lows that crippled you?

Is life more about being disappointed
than elevated,
or to search for hope,
faith and companionship?

As for me...

I've been a lover, a fighter
and a disgraceful motherfucker.
I've been there,
done that,
lived my life
and ain't afraid to go back for seconds...
as anything worth doing,
is worth overdoing and restraint is for the sensible and cowards.

I've talked to friends, strangers, murderers, addicts and therapists.
I've had enough booze and pussy to last 10 lifetimes,
so many drugs I should have died a 100 times...
but they never brought me happiness.

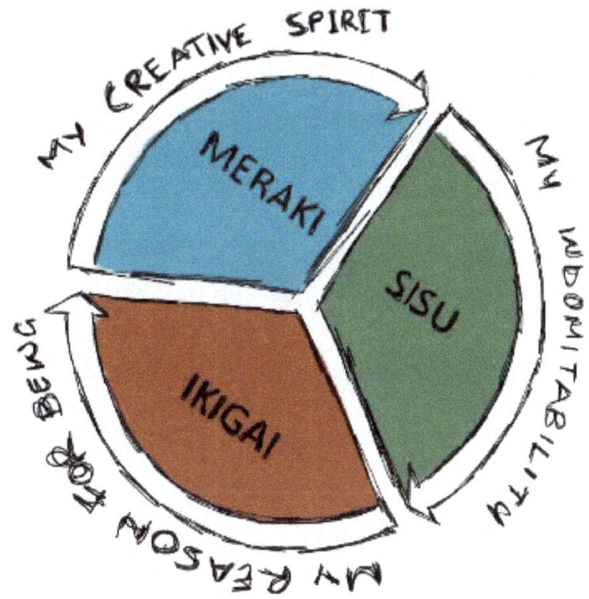

All I know...
that as a child the world seems so big.
When a teen,
no one understands you.
Twenties and thirties,
you'll conquer the globe.
At forty,
you finally understand that the world does not care,
but when fifty and sixty,
you grudgingly acknowledge the crushing disappointment and can be happy with what you've achieved against all the odds.

As you grow older,
the light fading,
accept death and be happy with those closest to you.

So, don't be middle of the road and keep it conservative.
There is no such thing, as,
knowing your place in the world –
you are the master of your destiny and captain of your pirate ship.

Embrace change,
challenge,
opportunity,
mistakes and failure;
go big or go home,
there isn't anything you can't do!

My kids are the centre of my life-
with them by my side there's no mountain too high to climb or sea too rough to swim.

Remember,
if you lose money… you really lose nothing,
if you lose your health… you lose something,
but if you lose your character… you lose everything!…

Live temet nosce.
Always look forward not back.
Be positive not negative.
And if you're in darkness,
find the light through embracing your sisu, ikigai and meraki so that when you go to the grave,
you can happily say:
I've willingly shared my journey and found happiness from others joining my rollercoaster and living my experience.

Outta my Control

Laptop crashing...
out of my control.

Nuclear armageddon...
out of my control.

The dog biting my football...
out of my control.

The ex...
out of my control.

How much I drink...
that's in my control,
I remind myself thus.

Price of a pint...
out of my control.

Who wins the FA Cup...
out of my control.

Future relationship with my kids...
partly in my control,
i remind myself thus.

Russian war crimes...
out of my control.

A pigeon shitting on me...
out of my control.

What I do next....
long term plans,
succeed or failure..
in my control,
I remind myself thus.

The next second, minute and
hour in my control...
to an extent,
I remind myself thus.

Slip on a banana skin,
fuck and sin,
wrists in handcuffs,
police pin,
mainly in my control...
I remind myself thus.

Winning on the pool table
dart board...
in my control.

The moon wanning,
tiding coming and going,
sun rising...
all out of my control,
I remind myself thus.

I'm stoical,
remember, what's in or out of my control,
I'll keep reminding myself thus.

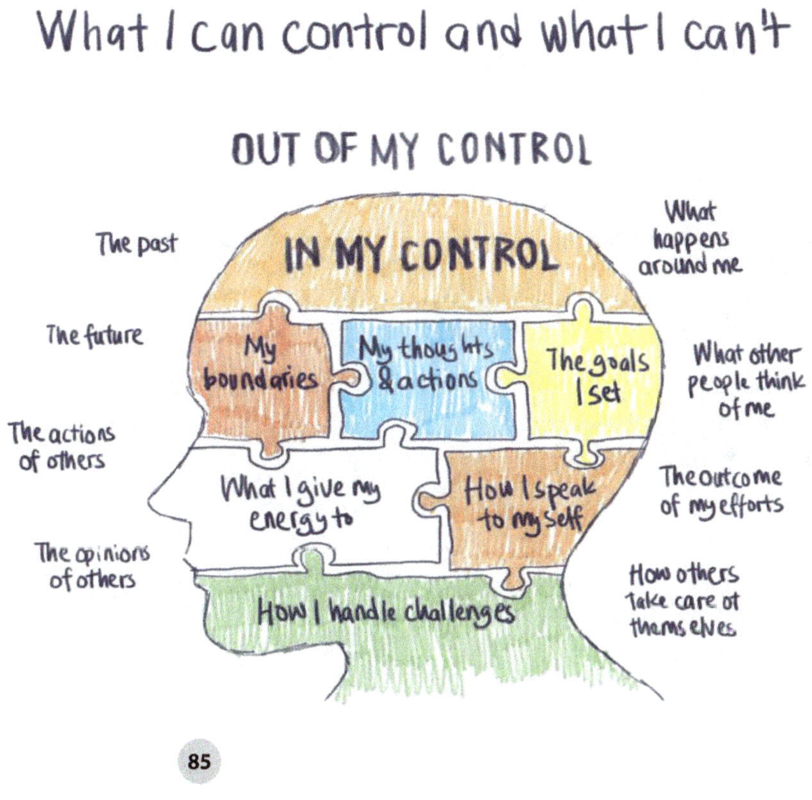

What I can control and what I can't

OUT OF MY CONTROL
IN MY CONTROL
My boundaries
My thoughts & actions
The goals I set
What I give my energy to
How I speak to myself
How I handle challenges
The past
The future
The actions of others
The opinions of others
What happens around me
What other people think of me
The outcome of my efforts
How others take care of themselves

This Life

You think it will be this,
but it's inevitably that,
sometimes good,
more often shat,
shit,
disappointment,
not what was expected or turned out.

This is what makes you,
defines your core beliefs,
what gives you relief,
identity prevails stronger than travails.

When you get knocked down,
get back up…
to get pushed down again,
to only hear defeat,
use that heat,
cussedness in your heart,
for success,
to prove the doubters,
haters,
useless wasters,
the wrongdoers all wrong.

Life is a funny thing,
bat shit crazy,
everyday an adventure,
50:50 good or bad,
never boring,
predictable.

Make life what you will,
bend energy to your force,
this is your personality,
how you design reality.

Lovebirds

Two women holding hands,
walking in love,
grey hairs signify their richness of life.

Their experience of ups and downs in this turbulent world,
only for them to know,
only they know what goes on behind closed doors,
the realities of their relationship.

Are they new lovers or have endured,
been battered and bruised,
but stuck together?

I watch them enjoy the day,
seeing the sights and experiencing the sun of their love as they go to another evening of carnival,
the experimentation of sights sounds and smells,
of living.

Another night of love not waning as they lie in each other arms,
enclosed in the embrace of love and friendship.

I look at these lovebirds,
think,
they look as happy as when they met,
maybe happier?

How did their lust change to love and understanding?
How do they manage this most difficult,
this most human of transitions?
Do they suffer will pangs of regret and jealousy?
Do they fight and shout,
scream and cry,
sulk and act petulantly?

Is their relationship sunny on the outside but complicated behind?

A life happy…
or miserable like mine;
with someone but feeling alone?

What does it make me when I see hope,
love,
truth and friendship,
and want it to end like a candle in the wind as I cry for the pain in my heart.

I'm no longer a clown full of jokes and laughter,
my heart now a stone,
devoid of expectation,
joy,
freedoms-
my thoughts dark.

What hope do I have when there's no one to rely on,
when my best friend,
my North Star lies,
deceives and manipulates to get her way?

I cry for the loss of our dream,
thunder when I see others in love.

I sit,
listen and admire my friends be who they are,
who they want to be...
honest...
their true selves.

I watch lovers,
see their song of passion,
love...
as they're in love,
excitement in each other.

I look on happy and sad....
happy for then,
sad for my jealousy as I barely hang on.

What life can I live separated from my children,
they turned against me?

This is an impossible life,
a parallel live,
a double life,
a life of sadness,
reflection,
hopelessness,
of giving up on trust.

Did I puts my desires above the common good,
the family;
what sort of a person am I?

I'm told that I'm selfish,
goal driven.
I'm misunderstood as I try to live free,
honest,
open as much as the old ladies;
I don't know what to think.

Hope,
love,
truth and friendship,
relationships are like a candle in the wind –
will it be blown out or start an inferno?

Such weighty questions of the heart and mind.
As George Edgin Pugh, a nuclear physicist, said,
if the human brain were so simple that we could understand it, we would be so simple that we couldn't.

Life really is a game of chess not chequers.
Chess,
16 pieces and a chequered board,
constant decisions,
champ or checkmate.
a game of strategy and tactics,
mental disintegration of the enemy,
holding nerve as you sacrifice pawns.

Life,
a game of chess not chequers.
What you do,
who you meet,
where you live,
whether to cross bridges or build fences.
When to make decisions and accept the consequences.
Needing to plan 20 steps ahead…
but willing to change at a moment's notice.
Keeping agile…
within a long-term strategy.
Being instinctive…
but not always trusting your gut.
Doing what your heart desires…
while reducing risks.

Life,
a game of chess not chequers.
love,
the game we all play,
one of truth or dare,
following your heart even when you brain says no.

Life,
being able to forgive,
having such hope only to be disappointed again and again,
not knowing when to call it a day,
even when in checkmate.

Family is part of the game of life.
Born into one,
leaving it as you make you way in the world,

then having your own only to leave when you die,
memories all that's left behind.

Work,
life's game of endurance.
Doing as you have no matter the tedium,
boredom,
bullying and stress;
toil ingrained in society.
Find your calling,
energy and passion,
inspiration;
work can be freedom in the great game.

A job,
something that will test me
thrill me,
excite and motivate me.
something I can feel pride in as a provider.

Friendships,
a game of snakes and ladders.
those who you trust,
share your intricacies,
rely on...
can stab you in the back.

Friends who you trust
share intricacies,
rely on…
can lift you to the heavens,
support all you do,
call out your silly shit and then reconcile.

Happiness,
a game of hide and seek.
So elusive,
confusing,
unreachable;
when you think you've found it,
joy can turn into unhappiness.

Adventure,
to explore new lands and languages,
smells and bodies,
tastes and temperaments,
life is a constant education to keep wanderlust in check,
to not let boredom become self-destructive tendencies.

I want more sex,
to give and receive pleasure or every sort,
no limitations or expectations,
try everything once.

I want a family
they my motivation to get out of bed and feel pride in the work I do,
to have adventures with as we make our journey through life.
They are those who will encourage me to cut down on the booze,
increase the exercise,
who I can support,
who will make me cry in happiness,
thankfulness and not those of a clown.

Life,
a game of chess not chequers,
an unending cycle of hope and happiness,
regret and disappointment,
positivity and negativity,
giving a shit then things getting fucked-up.

What do I want now,
this time in my life?
What is my next move,
what will make me get out of bed,
feel motivated,
fully anticipated and not constipated or castrated?

I need love, love, love.
we all do.
That special one who will pull you up when down,
make you smile when wanting to cry,
remind you,
tomorrow is another day and who knows what the tide might bring in.

I need my lovebird!

Be True to Thyself

We are born alone,
will die alone,
and now I'm here…
alone.

I try to be honest,
but honesty hurts,
I understand that.
I don't mean to pain,
unless the good sort.

What do you want me to do,
to say,
to be,
if not myself?

You have in your head something that's not there-
That's infatuation,
a different realisation,
new sensation,
I'm incomprehension.

Who do you think I am,
your hoped for visage or my reality?
A man with faults,
lives life large,
with laughter and love,
makes friends as quick as enemies,
but who lives free.

I need to be,
will be myself,
my own man.
I will live temet nosce,
not be fake news,
live a lie,
try to be what others want,
not who I am.

I will be transparent,
opening up not living in the shadows,
with this comes accountability,
responsibility,
hopefully not hypocrisy,
this, the burden of my truth.

I'm lost and unloved,
fate in my hands,
the choice to explore or bore,
mine alone.

I don't like this shit,
this not knowing,
world uncaring,
give me outcome unknown,
chance for life to get fucked up,
huge,
but feel alive-
life,
a tin of melted chocolate peanuts-
what you think you want is not always what you get,
cos,
if you aim for the grass you might tread in dog shit,
but,
if you shoot for the moon you will reach the stars.

I'll take my chances,
be the master of my destiny.
I've heard the siren call of adventure and excitement:
into the lion's den I will step,
believing.

I will accept responsibility for failures,
be accountable for screws-ups,
and rejoice in successes,
big or small,
whether tangible wealth or a smile from an unknown corner,
a similar soul also finding their way.

So,
here I am,
not knowing what the next week,
day or minute will bring,
and I'm ok with that.

I'll boss the universe,
proactively meet people soon to become friends,
I'll save for the day it rains and not let others,
those who are jealous,
cowards,
who think they're better than me,
get in my way;
we only have one life,
and this is my way of living.

So, I will walk into the night,
and if I get an offer,
a sketchy or gold-plated one,
imaginary or reality,
I will be open to excitement.

When I hear, yes,
whether lustful whisper or in the Tinder box,
an SMS from a number I don't know or email,
an invitation from any source,
is still an offer and I will accept.

And that is it.
End of poem,
end of my truth,
self–psychoanalysis hard reality.

I accept my desires,
needs and weaknesses,
cravings and addictions,
fears and hopes.

Know yourself,
be yourself,
don't be afraid of what others think of who or what you are,
who don't understand your fantasies or kinks

Remember,
no one has your back, but you!
Everyone else has their own shit to deal with,
they have enough to sort in their own life,
their own challenges,
their own troubles.

You are the last man in your garrison,
you will be manning the barricades, alone,
the hordes advancing,
surviving to the last bullet.

Only you can know what is in your head and

heart,
It is your nature and nurture,
your life experience.

At your death,
as you pass from this life to the other,
it will be your life that flashes though your mind,
your life reality,
your friends and enemies,
parents and children;
your truth.

It is only you that lives your life,
fuck anyone who tries to control you,
to circumnavigate or bastardise.
Others know nothing of where you have come from or going to.
It is your present,
your past,
your future.

The now is the now,
so live for it,
be yourself,
do the unexpected,
rejoice in the irrational and dangerous;
you'll not get a second chance.

When the pearly or fiery gates come into view,
think of what you have done and who you did it with.
Do not have regrets,
accept your mistakes and fuck ups,
this is the only way to be,
to live,
to love life as much as you should be understanding of yourself.

Be with those who care for you,
respect you,
love you,
for you being you…
and them being them.

Take them along for your ride…
but remember,
your life is your adventure as much as they have their own,
they just one part of yours,
you,
a small part of theirs.

This,
I believe,
the greatest gift,
to be honest with thy self,
to know thyself,
to live temet nosce,
to not be afraid,
to live truth.

Bucket List

A bucket list,
a combination of living an escape,
past and the future,
hope versus experience,
turning frog into prince,
wish or desire,
to fulfil something missing
need to be kissing,
cuddling,
feel like living…
for this is what it means to live your bucket list.

Throw yourself out of a plane,
jump from a bridge with bungee,
ski down mountains or scuba to the sea floor;
are these on your bucket list?

Cottage by the seaside,
see the northern lights,
touch an elephant,
a dog and two kittens;
are these on your bucket list?

Gamble in Vegas,
theatre in Leicester Square,
romance in Paris,
dine in Tokyo;
are these on your bucket list?

Threesomes,
foursomes,
gloryholes,
gangbangs and bukkakes;
are these on your bucket list?

Go to warzones,
cross the equator,
summit Everest,
swim with sharks;
are these on your bucket list?

Art in Florence,
club in Ibiza,
bridge in Sydney,
Jesus in Rio;
are these on your bucket list?

Crisp sandwich,
camp by the lake,
smile at the sun,
cavort in water;
are these on your bucket list?

Get married,
have kids,
reconcile with family,
life no longer on skids;
are these on your bucket list?

There is no right or wrong,
black or white,
each mind,

experience individual,
what we want, desire and crave, individual.

A bucket list,
a combination of living an escape,
past and the future,
hope versus experience,
turning frog into prince,
wish or desire,
to fulfil something missing
need to be kissing,
cuddling,
feel like living…
for this is what it means to live your bucket list.

Life

Normally hard,
unquestionably complicated,
an all-round motherfucker at times,
but choices-
give up and go home,
or go big,
a big fuck-off to living other's rules!

I call bullshit to any who doubt,
get in the way,
who are afraid of their shadow but give it the big'un;
you know the ones,
the wankers-
all talk no trouser!

This is life,
be the captain of your destiny,
steer your pirate ship,
dodge the cannon balls as you ride up through the valley of the shadow death;
guts or glory makes a damn good story.

Never give up wondering,
Exploring.
Find friendship,
partners.
Make own rules;
this is your life-
you only have one.

Cajones

There are times in life,
points of strife,
future unknown,
opportunity or challenge,
a hair breath separating the future,
success of failure.

You can't always make the right decision,
know all the 1,000 possible outcomes,
some be good others bad,
if you think about it too much,
you'll go mad.

What seems right,
move towards that light,
follow gut instinct,
keep it tight,
fight not flight,
enter the valley of the shadow of uncertainty…
in a certain way.

What will happen,
let it be,
you made a decision,
don't think revision.

Have strong spirit,
cajones in your hand,
certainty in your mind,
resolve in your heart…
make a choice.

Life Philosophy

Monday I'm broken,
Tuesday getting over,
Wednesday is hump day,
Thursday full of excitement,
Friday I'm alive,
Saturday the party continues,
Sunday no church for me.

Life is a rollercoaster,
on top of the world one moment,
in the depths next.

Monday I'm broken,
Tuesday getting over,
Wednesday is hump day,
Thursday full of excitement,
Friday I'm alive,
Saturday the party continues,
Sunday no church for me.

Sexuality,
others and yours,
maybe hard to understand...
but accept,
advise and support;
that's all you can give,
all you can expect to be given.

Monday I'm broken,
Tuesday getting over,
Wednesday is hump day,
Thursday full of excitement,
Friday I'm alive,
Saturday the party continues,
Sunday no church for me.

Teenage years,
the mind as much as body changing,
evolving,
trying to find equilibrium.
Working out what's normal,
how to fit into society,

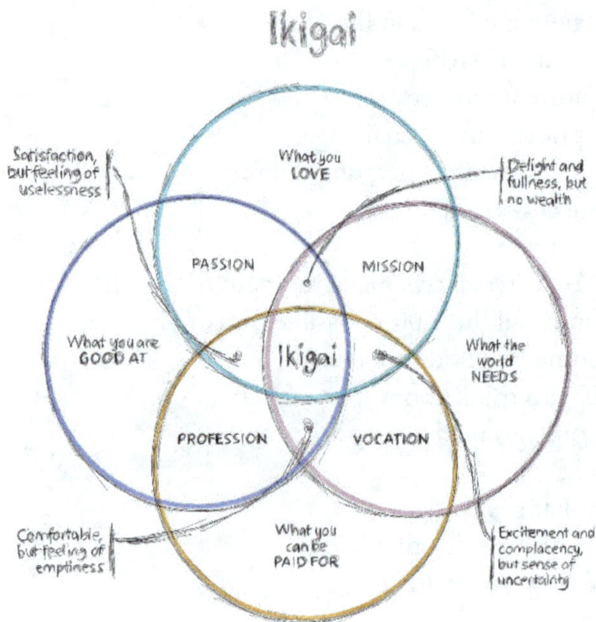

navigate the future,
who you are as a child,
sibling,
a human who should live their true self…
live temet nosce.

Monday I'm broken,
Tuesday getting over,
Wednesday is hump day,
Thursday full of excitement,
Friday I'm alive,
Saturday the party continues,
Sunday no church for me.

Life is complicated,
a rainbow,
not a yes or no world;
decisions are rarely black or white,
good and bad, never definite.

Monday I'm broken,
Tuesday getting over,
Wednesday is hump day,
Thursday full of excitement,
Friday I'm alive,

Saturday the party continues,
Sunday no church for me.

Life,
a thousand shades of in-between,
of what we make it.

The state,
society,
family and religion all influences,
but they do not,
should not dictate how a person lives;
only you can ask that question,
decide the answer.

Monday I'm broken,
Tuesday getting over,
Wednesday is hump day,
Thursday full of excitement,
Friday I'm alive,
Saturday the party continues,
Sunday no church for me.

Life is messy.
We can't,
shouldn't expect things to be perfect…
but find a path,
a way to navigate through it,
this the same for you,
as much as me.

Monday I'm broken,
Tuesday getting over,
Wednesday is hump day,
Thursday full of excitement,
Friday I'm alive,
Saturday the party continues,
Sunday no church for me.

Don't pressure yourself to be what others expect,
to conform,
but live the moment,
live your life and not someone's else's,
live your truth,
ride your rollercoaster.

Monday I'm broken,
Tuesday getting over,
Wednesday is hump day,
Thursday full of excitement,
Friday I'm alive,
Saturday the party continues,
Sunday no church for me.

The Present

Back to where was future,
past home,
very alone,
by self 14 months,
not living easy,
mind spaghetti,
marriage breakdown,
crying tears of a clown.

Revisiting ghosts five lifetimes later,
need a mental shelter,
bad memories coming,
here,
life I knew was ending,
I, not accepting,
became dead man walking,
too much talking in the head,
can't sleep when in bed,
brain not at rest,
subconscious working overtime,

That was yesteryear,
back now,
no emotional fear,
just realisation of times gone,
have to find new home,
hope,
I a pope,
someone to be preacher,
life renew reacher,
open mind stretcher,
new friend catcher,
this why new road walker,
nightmares, not be my stalker,
but motivational talker,
I, challenge the past,
put it where need to be as live present,
fast,
future still to make,
cake bake,
what went before made me who I am not who
I'll be!
As they say:
Yesterday, history,
tomorrow, a mystery.
today, a gift,
that's why it's called, the present.

Judgement

Will I learn from my past?
Will I be able to pass,
to articulate life lessons to my children so they don't fall into the same traps?

There is no time to waste,
friendship and love all that counts.

It's one step at a time;
clichés like hell,
but always move forward.

There is no time to waste,
friendship and love all that counts.

I'm not here to judge so don't judge me.
I'm not you nor you me,
we,
should both be positivity,
this, the way to be.

There is no time to waste,
friendship and love all that counts.

Tackle each situation on its merits however fucked they might be.
Realise,
they are my decisions and mistakes,
I'm accountable for my actions,
my choices are mine alone.

There is no time to waste,
friendship and love all that counts.

The best laid plans of mice and men often go a glade-
we must but rise above the chaos,
each day a stride not sprint.
Calculate the best outcomes,
the 51% choice over the 49,
both having positives and negatives.

There is no time to waste,
friendship and love all that counts.

Your choice if predictable,
doesn't always mean reliable,
sensible,
estimable,
unremarkable...
it can be most interesting,
don't let it be mind festering,
life philosophy altering.

There is no time to waste,
friendship and love all that counts.

We each have a life to lead,
immeasurable equations to handle,
no point throwing stones in glass houses,
but rather support and understand life's ambiguities.

There is no time to waste,
friendship and love all that counts.

Riding the Tempest

When I left,
my mind a right old mess,
spaghetti,
not sure which direction I was going in,
all certainties taken from me...
father to the grave,
children to place unknown,
financially fucked,
family house into internet zone,
work…
out of the fire into frying pan,
I had no plan,
no certainty of what to do or who I was.

It was a time of mental degradation,
emotional hibernation,
fire-fighting and psychological damage limitation,
passing out the storm and battening down the hatches while waiting for Spring.

I needed peace,
introspection,
contemplation,
anger exfoliation.

Questioning, who I was and what I would do,
only possible without all the noise around,
this, I thought, lead to redemption,
mental reinvigoration.

So, I said,
fuck, suicide nation,
that never on the menu...
but when you don't know yourself,
the mind wandering,
no good outcomes seen,
thoughts pass,
needed to battle through,
find positives out of negatives,
be reminded wonders of the natural world,
glorious views,
epic scenery,
mainly by self,
but few new friends found and old ones supported.

I just needing time,
working out a plan,
a way forward,
finding my sister,
a guardian angel I didn't know,
seeing sights never to be forgotten,
experiences had,
no more feeling sad.

Uncertainties still there,
now, just on my list to do.
It's time to kick ass again,
I, leaving the shelter,

mental bunker,
once more to knock down doors and take on the world...
as where there's a will...
and there is a fucking will,
there is a way…
and I will find the fucking way!

Fate once more in my hands,
time to bury that negativity,
uncertainty and shake it up as its always darkest before the dawn,
I still a life pirate and captain of my ship.

I will keep aiming for the moon so as to hit the stars,
the best pilots finding a way to navigate the choppiest seas,
the greater the challenge
the more than man reveals himself as I've not been looking for peace,
but to find my old self so I can take on new challenges and get back in the game!
As, when I think it,
I will say then do it;
doing nothing,
impossible,
giving up…
mentally reprehensible!

Living

Living is living,
dramatizing and fantasising,
dancing and scratching.

Living is living,
driving and flying,
diving and paragliding.

Living is living,
conspiring and freewheeling,
biting and drinking.

Living is living,
slapping and fucking,
fighting and loving,
commiserating and celebrating,
arguing and partnering,
destroying and building,
this is living.

Living is living,
crying and laughing,
joking and poking,
punching and hugging,
We all living,
finding,
exploring,
making it through life one day at a time;
this is living.

Bittersweet

We all have life,
sugar and spice,
bittersweet,
angels and demons-
living,
strawberries and lemons.

The sweet,
killed by sour,
a love,
dying hour-by-hour.

A friendship,
thought forever kinship,
ends in hateship…
that ship,
sunk!

Don't know where they are,
what doing,
if ok…
who screwing.

Now moving forward,
not backward,
mentally free,
my life,
have to be,
looking outward.

Yesterday, history,
Tomorrow, a wonderful mystery.

We all have life,
sugar and spice,
bittersweet,
angels and demons-
living,
strawberries and lemons.

A FINAL THOUGHT

No one can predict the future; I certainly have no idea what will unfold. However, I don't believe in the have it all illusion. I have come to reject the notion, success and wellbeing should religiously follow the happiness myth of needing financial wealth, a fancy job title and marriage. That we shouldn't follow the endless bombardment of corporate advertising telling us to hoard material objects. But rather, it's fine to reject conventional expectations. You don't need to be ambitious, educated, wealthy or successful. You don't have to get married, be monogamous and have a house full of kids. It's ok to have a little bit of devil in your life and not follow all of society's written and unwritten rules. True contentment lies in embracing our individuality and live on one's own terms. The more money you have doesn't correlate to being happier; that's codswallop. It's time with family and friends and not net wealth that's truly important. Money is just as addictive and destructive as heroin, fags, sex, booze and cake. When you stop trying to catch an impossible shadow it's tremendously liberating. It allows us to discover our own sources of contentment and fulfilment.

So, what can make you content, bring joy and meaning to life; what's the elixir of life? It varies for each individual. I consider myself happy. While I'm divorced I now live by my rules rather than those articulated by government, religion, family or my ex-wife. I have received a lot of painful (and expensive) life lessons. One thing in common they all had: the observance to societal power structures and rules, laws and norms which embed the advantages of the elite and has next to nothing to do with my core beliefs. I'm now more mentally free from such expectations. Failure is not a reason to be disheartened but an opportunity for growth and resilience. Taking risks, trying something new, and refusing to be deterred by the opinions of others, can be empowering and inspiring.

I have learned to try new things and I'm prepared to be rubbish at them. So, don't get disheartened if you fail, but try, try… and try again. People might laugh… but they will likely secretly admire you for taking a risk they weren't willing to. If it was wonky, ugly but fun, it was probably worth it. Set low goals and standards and then slowly raise the bar, this allows you to chart your own course. While it's important to have a destination in mind, it's equally vital to savour the journey. You will eventually reach your goal. So, don't get frustrated by the twists and turns in life. And never say, you can't. Decide what you want and everything else will fall into place.

And think about death, contemplate your mortality. If you die tomorrow, have you led a good life? Will you be at peace as you take your last breath? Will you be remembered as a champion person or a bit of a bastard? More importantly, it's not about being remembered as saint or scoundrel but rather finding balance in the complexities of being a human!

Lastly, define what success means to you. It doesn't need to be the size of your bank account but rather the legacy you leave behind or, what makes you content; define your own terms. Working a small plot of land as part of a community to grow veggies and raising a puppy is what can give a sense of success, purpose. It's friends and family I thank and admire most. I love our shared appreciation of silliness and venerate their steadfast support; I hope they feel the same about me. There is no universal right or wrong when it comes to defining success; it's a personal journey. My objective, establish a philosophy of how to reach high points and to fully embrace sisu, ikigai and meraki as my life continues its rollercoaster.

Thank you, dear reader, my friend for being on this poetic journey. I hope through my experiences I have given you a new perspective on life. So, I say, never blame your circumstances. A positive mind-set will always lead to a more fortuitous outcome than a negative approach. One should not fear failure; it happens- get up and give it another lash. Don't be ashamed of your mistakes; learn from them. We all screw-up, accept this is part of life. Embrace experience, good or bad; there is always something to be learned. If you don't go after what you want, you will never have it. If you don't ask, the answer is always no. If you don't step forward, you will remain in the same place. Be curious and have a willingness to engage with the unknown. Questioning does not show weakness but is rather a sign of strength, a true measure of intelligence. Open yourself to the world and express that you aren't afraid to exhibit your ignorance but want to learn, search for knowledge and truth from those who can educate and guide. "By doubting we are led to question, by questioning we arrive at the truth." Peter Abelard, 1079- 1142

My Way

My time is near,
soon, no more sunsets.
Regrets,
I have a few,
smiles,
even more so;
I've always done it my way.

You might not agree with what I've done-
rules broken,
hearts destroyed,
goals reached…
more rules broken;
always doing it my way.

I've lived a full life,
seen the world,
been high as a kite and low as a whale;
always living my way.

Celebrated successes,
commiserated failures,
both too many to mention;
I've lived my life and done it my way

Family I was born to,
loves, I've had a few.
friends, many a comrade,
enemies, firing cross and bow.

I've lived and will die,
MY WAY.

ABOUT THE AUTHOR

I'm an entrepreneur & business consultant by day, novelist & poet by night. The son of a British Army officer, I volunteered in rural Tanzania in 1997 before going to university to study marketing. I have lived and worked in Ethiopia, Germany, Kenya, Jordan, Ireland, Malawi, Saudi Arabia, Tanzania and the UK over the last 25 years, my varied experiences of culture, relationships, food, music and everything else that makes the world go round, the source of my inspiration.

www.ingramcontent.com/pod-product-compliance
Lightning Source LLC
LaVergne TN
LVHW080332110826
845155LV00024B/149

* 9 7 8 1 9 1 6 1 8 6 7 7 4 *